Presented To

By

Occasion

---

*f*P

IT'S YOUR TIME

JOURNAL

A Guide to Activating Your Faith,
Achieving Your Dreams,
and Increasing in God's Favor

JOEL OSTEEN

FREE PRESS

New York London Toronto Sydney

A Division of Simon & Schuster, Inc.
1230 Avenue of the Americas
New York, NY 10020

First Free Press hardcover edition December 2010

FREE PRESS and colophon are trademarks of Simon & Schuster, Inc.

For information about special discounts for bulk purchases,
please contact Simon & Schuster Special Sales at
1-800-456-6798 or business@simonandschuster.com

Manufactured in the United States of America

3   5   7   9   10   8   6   4   2

ISBN: 978-1-4516-0989-9
ISBN: 978-1-4516-1040-6 (ebook)

CONTENTS

STEP THREE:
IT'S TIME FOR RESTORATION

STEP FOUR:
IT'S TIME TO TRUST

STEP FIVE:
IT'S TIME TO STRETCH

INTRODUCTION

*I*t's *Your Time* was written to build faith in the lives of those in need of encouragement by calling forth the seeds of greatness that God planted within. We'd come through some challenging times as a nation and as individuals, so I wanted to offer the hope and assurances that there were better days ahead. This journal based on *It's Your Time* contains that same hope-filled message in a more intimate form, inviting readers to add their own daily thoughts and prayers.

My prayer, as always, is that I can inspire you, build your faith, and expand your vision so you might find the courage to overcome obstacles, accomplish your dreams, and increase God's favor in your life. In Scriptures, God promises that He will not withhold what you need to become what He created you to be as long as you walk uprightly. This journal offers encouragement every step of the way in that walk. It is designed to help you live with purpose and passion and the desire to help others.

Millions of individuals and families were adversely affected by the economic downturn that resulted in shutdowns, layoffs, foreclosures, and lost assets for people of all ages and incomes. Relationships have been badly stressed. We've all needed God's help to weather this storm. Many are still struggling to get back on their feet.

Whatever your challenges, this journal is intended to help you help yourself to find as much encouragement and inspiration as you need. My words are on the page, but feel free to add your own thoughts in the margins, on the lines, whenever they come to you, however they can help you. The following pages offer a number of tools for lifting your spirits and building your faith. You'll find Scriptures, selected stories, sections from *It's Your Time*, and thoughts and prayers intended to help you focus your heart, mind, and energies on positive steps toward your goals and your God-given destiny.

Find a place of solitude, away from televisions and traffic and the daily distractions that can make meditation and contemplation difficult if not impossible. Mentally peel the stress away before entering the sanctuary these pages provide. I've left plenty of space for you to add your own thoughts and self-encouragements so that we can work as a team. This book is designed as a daily journal, so there is no need to rush through it. Take your time, build your strength, and bolster your faith one day at a time. It gives you a five-week serving of daily reading, reflection, and encouragement. Once you've gone through it, feel free to begin again. Allow time to let the encouraging words sink in and replenish your spirits. As always, listen for the still, small voice of God's grace and direction. Add your own responses as you go, because when you write them down, it helps reinforce the positive messages, building your resolve to keep moving forward, fortified in your faith that your time has come. Putting your thoughts on paper also helps you to self-analyze and self-correct so that you can continue on course to your dreams. Finally, when you add your own entries, this journal can serve as a record of your progress as God puts His hands atop yours, adds His strength to your own, stepping in, lifting up, giving freely of His love to you, His child.

I give you permission to write without concern about spelling or grammar. You won't be graded or judged. There are no right or wrong responses. You should feel free to enter your thoughts, measure them, reconsider, revise, and rewrite. Be honest, stay focused, and soak up as much encouragement as you can. Do your best, and God will do the rest.

My dream is that one day this journal will serve as a chronicle and testimony of your walk in faith. I would love for it to become a record of your entering a time when all that you've invested and all that God has created will bear fruit beyond your wildest dreams. Keep your heart pure, strive for excellence, and prepare yourself, because it's your time for God's goodness, favor, and restoration. It's your time to walk in the fullness of His blessing.

Step One

It's Time to Believe

This section is entitled "It's Time to Believe," because tough times require strong faith, because your current challenges will pass, because big problems precede bigger things to come, because every disappointment gives us fresh opportunities, and because each season of scarcity gives way to new seasons of increase.

As you begin this journal chapter, know that it's time to reaffirm your belief in the fact that you are one of our Father's children. You are made in His image, and He loves you!

DAY 1

ASK GOD TO LIGHT YOUR PATH

KEY TRUTH: Your gifts can get you there.

Amber Corson was a stay-at-home mom with three young children. When her husband was laid off from his Florida construction job as the economy soured, Amber had to take a night-shift job to help support the family.

She'd been working that late shift for four weeks. One night she was driving home, tired, scared, missing her kids, and worried about their future. Amber felt like God had bigger plans for her family than to struggle like this. She prayed on that drive home: "God, please tell me what I can do to get my family through this."

She said His response came to her "like a breath."

"I gave you a gift. Go plant gardens. Do your heart's work."

Amber had a degree in horticulture that she'd never used. She was so talented she'd been certified as a master gardener. She had a natural talent for making things grow. That night, she told her husband what God had put in her heart. She prayed on it. In the next few weeks, she said, things "just fell into place like it had been planned for me all along."

She called her landscaping business Eden Paradise Gardens. It grew quickly and flourished beyond anything she had dreamed. It was her time!

A global recession has forced many to postpone their dreams and cancel their plans. You may have lost your job. You may have lost your savings, maybe even your home. It could be that you have health concerns or relationships problems. Maybe you are frustrated because it's taking so long to get where you want to be in your life. Yet now is not the time to talk yourself out of your goals and dreams. Now is not the time to get discouraged. You may think that you're not even halfway there. You may feel you have so far to go. But the truth is, you don't know. Your dream may just be up around the corner. You may think it will take another two years. But if you stay in faith, who knows? It may just be two more months. You are closer than you think.

God wants to breathe new life into your dreams. He wants to breathe new hope into your heart. You may be about to give up on a marriage, on a troubled child, on a lifelong goal. But God wants you to hold on. He says that if you'll get your second wind, if you'll put on a new attitude and press forward like you're headed down the final stretch, you'll see Him begin to do amazing things.

CONSIDER THIS: You need to tune out the negative messages. Quit telling yourself: *I'm never landing back on my feet financially. I'm never breaking this addiction. I'm never landing a better job.* Instead, your declarations should be: *I am closer than I think. I can raise this child. I can overcome this sickness. I can make this business work. I know I can find a new job.* You must get up each day knowing this could be the day you get the break you need. This could be the day you see your health turn around. This could be the day your child comes back home. This could be the day you meet the man or woman of your dreams.

Lord, grant that I might
always desire more than
I can accomplish.

—*Michelangelo*

WHAT THE SCRIPTURES SAY

For his anger lasts only a moment,
but his favor lasts a lifetime;
weeping may remain for a night,
but rejoicing comes in the morning.
—*Psalm 30:5 (NIV)*

Return to your fortress, O prisoners of hope; even now I announce
that I will restore twice as much to you.
—*Zechariah 9:12 (NIV)*

A PRAYER FOR TODAY

Father in heaven, thank You for giving me Your gifts. I open my heart to You and receive Your perfect love. Fill me with Your confidence and the assurance to embrace everything You have for me.

Life must be lived forward, but can only be understood backward.

—*Søren Kierkegaard*

TAKEAWAY TRUTH: My gifts have been planted in me permanently by God. When I stay in faith and trust in those gifts, I move closer to achieving my goals and fulfilling my God-given destiny.

DAY 2

STAY STRONG
FOR THE FINAL PUSH

KEY TRUTH: The greatest difficulty always comes right before the birth of a dream.

A couple I know told me their son was on the wrong path, running with the wrong crowd. He had addictions he needed to overcome. They were doing everything they could to help him. They found him a new place to live away from his drug-using friends. They found a support group for him. They were praying more than ever. But they said, "Joel, it seems like the more we pray, the more we try, the more we believe, the worse he gets."

They were so concerned. But I told them what I'm telling you. The reason the pressure has been turned up is because you're close to your victory. The enemy would not be fighting so hard if he didn't know he was about to lose his grip on this child.

If you will keep believing, keep hoping, keep doing the right thing, and if you stay strong for that final push, you will see the situation turn around. You'll see that promise come to pass.

It's just like a woman having a baby. The first month or two is not that difficult. No big deal. The mother-to-be looks and feels much the same. But then in a few months she gains the baby's weight. She carries around the extra pounds. Her feet may swell up. Her back may hurt. She may have some nausea, some morning sickness.

By the eighth or the ninth month, husbands, you know you'd better give that woman some space. Don't mess with Momma. Don't backtalk her. Just do what she says and nobody will get hurt. She gets more and more uncomfortable. But then when her water breaks and she goes into labor, all those other challenges seem insignificant compared to the difficulty of giving birth.

When Victoria was in labor with our first child, our son Jonathan, she was holding on to my arm so tight. When she had a contraction, she squeezed my arm. Victoria would scream, and then I would scream.

I wanted to mention to her that she was hurting me, but I feared for my life!

Truth be told, if a woman in labor had a choice, she'd probably say, "I don't want to do this anymore. It's too difficult. I can't stand it."

But she doesn't have a choice. The doctor, the nurse, the husband keep saying, "Push! Push! Push!" Before long, she pushes that baby out. And in a few minutes she forgets all about the pain because she's holding the promise. She's holding that little child.

It's the same principle in dealing with daily life. The greatest difficulty always comes right before the birth of a dream. Before you see a new level of God's favor, don't be surprised if things come against you to try to discourage you. People may try to talk you out of your dreams, to convince you to just settle where you are.

You may not realize that you are "in labor" right now. You are about to give birth to what God has put in your heart. That's why it's such a struggle. You're in that final push. Maybe at work you're doing the right thing, going the extra mile, but you were passed over for a promotion. It wasn't fair. What was that disappointment? A labor pain. So just push through it.

Maybe you wanted to create that new business, but your partner backed out. The financing didn't come through. What was that disappointment? Another labor pain. If you'll keep pushing, keep believing, keep hoping, before long—like that woman— you will push that promise out.

CONSIDER THIS: You may feel as though you've never had such a struggle, in your finances, your health, or your relationships. You could say, "Joel, this is the greatest attack that I've ever faced." Instead of getting down and thinking, *Poor old me,* learn to turn it around and say, "Yes, this is the greatest attack that I've ever been through, but I know it means that I'm headed for the greatest victory that I've ever seen." Remember, it's always darkest right before the dawn.

_____

_____

_____   ⸋

_____   What would you attempt
                                     to do if you knew you
_____   would not fail?

_____   —*Robert H. Schuller*

_____

_____

_____

WHAT THE SCRIPTURES SAY

I can do all things through Christ who strengthens me.
—*Philippians 4:13 (WEB)*

Fear not, for I *am* with you;
Be not dismayed, for I *am* your God.
I will strengthen you,
Yes, I will help you,
I will uphold you with My righteous right hand.'
—*Isaiah 41:10 (NKJ)*

A PRAYER FOR TODAY

Father God, thank You for giving me power to push past fear. I choose to move beyond fear and toward the destiny You have chosen for me. Thank You for showing me any areas of my life where fear is holding me back so that I can push forward into the life of victory You have for me.

A little more persistence, a little more effort, and what seemed hopeless failure may turn to glorious success.

—*Elbert Hubbard*

TAKEAWAY TRUTH: I'm about to give birth to my promise.

DAY 3

YOUR DAY IS COMING

KEY TRUTH: Even though it may take a long time, God always has a way to bring your dream to pass.

In a study on the power of attitude, researchers wanted to see how rats' attitudes affected their will to live. They put one rat in a large tub of water with high sides so he could not get out. Then they put the tub in a dark room. They timed how long the rat would keep swimming before he gave up. The rat lasted a little over three minutes.

Then the researchers put another rat in the same tub, but this time they allowed a bright ray of light to shine into the room. That rat swam more than thirty-six hours, seven hundred times longer than the rat with no light.

Why was that? The rat with no light had no hope. When he looked ahead, he saw only darkness. There wasn't any reason to keep swimming. That's what happens when we don't expect God's favor. We lose faith that we can overcome our obstacles. We don't believe that God is in control, so we lose our passion, we lose our enthusiasm.

Remember that whenever challenges arise and your stress levels soar, that's a sign that your time is near. When negative thoughts bombard your mind, when you are most likely to be discouraged, and when you feel like giving up on your dreams—that's *not* the time to give up. That's *not* the time to throw in the towel. That's the time to adjust your attitude to a more positive one. You are closer than you think.

Don't allow yourself to become a prisoner of fear and doubt. You'll know that this is happening when you have inner thoughts like: *Nothing good ever happens to me. It's never changing, Joel. It's just been too long.*

Break away from negative thoughts. Free yourself with the gift of hope. No matter how long it takes, no matter how impossible it looks, your attitude should be: "I just can't help it. I know it will work out. I know I will overcome. It may be taking a long time, but I know this too shall pass. It may be difficult, but I know that means I'm close to my victory."

The Scripture says, "We walk by faith and not by sight." That means we don't have to see it to believe it. It's just the opposite. If we believe it, *then* we see it.

Take your dreams and the promises God has put in your heart and every day declare that they will come to pass. Just say something like, "Father, I want to thank You that my payday is coming. You said no good thing will You withhold because I walk uprightly. And I believe even right now You are arranging things in my favor."

We all have goals we want to accomplish and situations we believe we will turn around. But often when it's taking a long time and things are not working out, it's easy to lose our enthusiasm. If you listen to negative thoughts, you will likely become discouraged and give up on your dreams. Many times we miss out on God's best because we give up too soon. We don't realize how close we are to victory.

Hold on to your faith. Another few days of believing, another few weeks of doing the right thing, or another few months of staying in faith and you will see that promise come to pass.

Right now, you are so close to seeing that situation turn around. That answer you've been praying about is just right around the corner. You can't afford to get discouraged. You can't afford to give up now.

You may have doubts when your troubles seem to pile up. I realize that sometimes it seems like the more you pray, the worse things become. Even when you do the right thing, you may be blindsided by the wrong results. In those cases, the easy thing would be to say, "Forget it. I don't have to put up with this." "This marriage never will work." "I'll never be able to raise this child." "I don't like this job."

Instead of being discouraged, be persistent. Announce: "I've come too far to stop now. I've been through too much to back down. I realize the pressure has been turned up because I'm about to give birth to my dreams!"

CONSIDER THIS: It's important to keep reminding yourself: "The Creator of the universe is directing my steps. He has me in the palm of His hands. And even though this is difficult, I know it's just a matter of time before it turns around. I know my payday is coming." You may be about to give up on a dream. You think it's been too long. It never will change. It will never work out. But you must get your fire back. Fan that flame. Keep that dream alive. Even though it's taking a long time, the good news is, God still has a way to bring it to pass.

_____

_____

_____

_____

_____

———— ⧉ ————   _____

_____

Sorrow looks back, worry   _____
looks around, faith looks up.
_____
—*Unknown*
_____

_____

_____

_____

WHAT THE SCRIPTURES SAY

We can rejoice, too, when we run into problems and trials, for we
know that they help us develop endurance. And endurance develops strength of character, and character strengthens our confident hope of salvation.

—*Romans 5:3–4 (NLT)*

Wait on the LORD: be of good courage, and he shall strengthen
thine heart: wait, I say, on the LORD.

—*Psalm 27:14 (KJV)*

A PRAYER FOR TODAY

Lord, You are a loving, merciful, forgiving God. Thank You for
strengthening my heart, building my character, and putting confidence in my soul.

_____

_____

_____   ❧

_____   Help thyself and God
                                     will help thee.
_____
                                   —*George Herbert*
_____

_____

_____

_____

_____

_____

_____

TAKEAWAY TRUTH: I may not be able to control the negative things that happen to me, but I can pray to my heavenly Father for the strength to control my response to those things and to take even the bad and use it as a force for good in my life with His help and guidance.

DAY 4

GOD WILL BRING YOUR DREAMS TO PASS

KEY TRUTH: God has all kinds of ways to bring your dreams to pass.

A young couple from our church told me about the challenges they had while trying to sell their house. They had only a few prospects in the first few weeks. They weren't having much luck.

The market was tough. Realtors told them it may take six months, a year, maybe even two years to sell. But this couple had an attitude of faith. They were prisoners of hope. And even though it didn't look good, they kept reminding themselves, "We are closer than we think. It could happen any day."

This one couple came back to look at the house a second time. They wanted to spend a couple of hours really studying it to see if it was right for their family. The owners were okay with that. But they debated whether they should take down their personal pictures of themselves and their children, just so they could remain more private. After they thought about it, they felt good about leaving those pictures where they were.

The potential buyers came to look at the house, and the owners left so they could take their time. A few hours later, they received a call from the real estate agent saying the couple definitely wanted to purchase the house. The buyers told my friends that they'd been torn between their house and another one. But during that last visit, they'd seen something that convinced them to buy my friends' house.

"We saw a picture of you and your pastor, and we thought: 'These people love God. They go to Lakewood. This must be the house for us!' "

My friend told me: "Joel, you helped me sell my house."

I told him that was great. "Now let's talk about my commission."

God can cause a simple photograph to be in the right place at the right time to help you.

God is in complete control. So be a prisoner of hope. Get up each day expecting His favor. Hear my message: God is breathing new life into your dreams. You will feel the wind of His spirit lift your sails once again. You are not meant to simply endure life. Barely getting by is not acceptable. You were meant to dance on top of the waves.

More challenges mean you're closer to your victory. Don't give up on your dream. Don't give up your relationship because the waters get rough. Don't give up on living a healthy life because illness brings you down. Times may grow tough, but remember there are rewards for staying in faith.

God promises your payday is on its way. If you'll learn to be a prisoner of hope and get up every day expecting God's favor, you'll see God do amazing things. You'll overcome every obstacle. You'll defeat every enemy. And I believe and declare you'll see every dream, every promise God has put in your heart, come to pass.

CONSIDER THIS: When negative thoughts come and your burden seems so heavy you feel discouraged, just keep telling yourself: "I'm closer than I think. Right now the Creator of the universe is lining up things in my favor: the right people, the right breaks, the right opportunities." Maybe you have been through tough times. Resolve to move forward. Don't stay there. Put on a new attitude. Disappointments come and go, but God's favor is for a lifetime.

_____

_____

_____

_____

_____

_____

_____

Attitude is a little thing that makes a big difference.

—*Winston Churchill*

_____

_____

_____

_____

_____

_____

_____

_____

_____

_____

_____

WHAT THE SCRIPTURES SAY

> When my spirit grows faint within me,
> it is you who know my way.
> In the path where I walk
> men have hidden a snare for me.
>
> —*Psalm 142:3 (NIV)*

Joyful are those who listen to me, watching for me daily at my gates, waiting for me outside my home!

—*Proverbs 8:34 (NLT)*

A PRAYER FOR TODAY

Father, help me to understand that when I cannot find a way, You can, and that when I cannot make a way, You can. Teach me to always have faith in You.

_____

_____

He who has so little
knowledge of human nature
as to seek happiness by
changing anything but his
own disposition will waste
his life in fruitless efforts.

—*Samuel Johnson*

_____

_____

_____

_____

_____

_____

_____

_____

TAKEAWAY TRUTH: When faced with challenges, I need to stay in faith so that my Father in heaven can step in and provide for me so that I can live up to His expectations.

DAY 5

A GOOD LIFE
ATTRACTS GOOD THINGS

KEY TRUTH: The seeds you plant will lead to a harvest you can't imagine.

For more than forty years, the church custodian known as Mister John offered his fix-it skills to help others in a small Florida town. He and his wife Laverne, the church secretary, were the town's good Samaritans. They didn't have much, but they were the people to call if your fence needed fixing, your car broke down, or your kids needed clothes for school.

Then suddenly the tables were turned. A few years after Mister John and Laverne retired from their church jobs, a fire broke out in their old wood-frame cottage. Half of their humble home was destroyed.

Things did not turn for the better in the days that followed. Before the couple could salvage what remained of their belongings, thieves broke in. They ripped out the copper plumbing and flooded what was left of the house, destroying everything in it.

A friend offered the couple a place to stay for as long as they needed it, but there wasn't enough insurance money to rebuild their longtime home. People were kind and offered to help but the recession had left many in their town unemployed, struggling to get by. Mister John and Laverne did not want to add to anyone's burden by asking for more than others could afford to give.

What they didn't realize was that it was their time. It was their time to reap the rewards of their faith, kindness, and unselfishness. After so many years of blessing others, it was their time to be blessed.

Mister John and Laverne didn't have to ask for help. Friends and neighbors simply showed up one by one. They pitched in, offering money, food, furniture, clothing, a place to stay.

Then a local builder came forward. His business had slowed some, too, but he'd done well over the years building luxury homes. And he had never forgotten that twenty years earlier, as a teenage volunteer at his church, he'd been taught basic carpentry skills by the kindly Mister John.

"I've been waiting all my life to repay him," the builder said.

To do that, the builder recruited an architect, roofers, plumbers, electricians, carpenters, and other tradespeople. They built Mister John and Laverne a new home nearly twice the size of their old one. They donated their time and materials, and they raised money to pay for what the insurance did not cover. When the grateful elderly couple moved into their beautiful new cottage, they called it "the house that love built."

God has a way even when it looks like there is no way. God has put promises in every heart. You have dreams and desires, things you want to accomplish, situations you want to see changed. So often, you gave up on those dreams, because it took so long, or because you tried and failed, or because you went through a disappointment, or because somebody didn't treat you right.

You may have become complacent. Maybe you are not pursuing what God has put in your heart. But I want to encourage you today to get your fire back. You have to stay filled with hope. It may be taking a long time, but God is a faithful God. He is saying that no matter how long it's been, no matter how impossible it looks, if you'll stay in faith, your time is coming.

Every dream that's in your heart, every promise that has taken root, God not only put there but has every intention of bringing to pass. I want you to have this attitude: *My time is coming. I've been giving and giving. I haven't seen a lot of results, but that's okay. I know my time is coming.*

Maybe you are living in a small apartment and all of your friends have nice homes. This attitude will serve you: *I'm not discouraged. I know my time is coming.*

Maybe you really want to get married but haven't met the right person. Take this attitude: *I know God's in control. At the right time He will bring the right person. My time is coming.*

This is what hope is all about—*believing that the promise God put in you will come to pass.* I love that David says he pitched his tent in the land of hope. Where have you pitched your tent? What are you expecting each day? What kind of attitude do you have?

Some might say, "I've been praying for my child for five years. I don't think he ever will change."

Or "Everybody on my job gets promoted except me."

Or even "I tried to launch this business, but nobody would help me."

In each of these responses, the tent has been pitched in the wrong place. Move out of the "Not Going to Happen" subdivision. Move out of "Can't-Do-It-Ville." Leave "Self-Pity Estates." Get out of those dead-end neighborhoods and move into a land of hope, a land of faith, a land where you know anything is possible, a place where you know your time is coming.

CONSIDER THIS: You must believe for God's blessings and favor. You must expect God to turn things around. You need to go dig up your stakes, pack up your belongings, and move out of the land of discouragement. Instead, set up camp in the Land of the Believers. Find people of faith and surround yourself with those who inspire and encourage you.

The only disability in
life is a bad attitude.

—*Scott Hamilton*

WHAT THE SCRIPTURES SAY

So do not throw away your confidence; it will be richly rewarded. You need to persevere so that when you have done the will of God, you will receive what he has promised. For in just a very little while, "He who is coming will come and will not delay.

—Hebrews 10:35–37 (NIV)

Let us not be weary in well doing: for in due season we shall reap, if we faint not.

—Galatians 6:9 (KJV)

A PRAYER FOR TODAY

Father, thank you for the dream You put in my heart and for allowing Your promise to take root. Help me to stay in faith and to overcome challenges so that I can fulfill the plan You created for my life.

In the depth of winter I
finally learned that there was
in me an invincible summer.

—Albert Camus

_____

_____

_____

_____

_____

_____

_____

TAKEAWAY TRUTH: I must do my best to stay positive and to see the challenges that come in my life as opportunities to build character and prove my faith in God's divine goodness.

DAY 6

THERE IS SOMETHING ABOUT
A PERSON FILLED WITH HOPE

KEY TRUTH: Stay in faith, and God will get you to where you need to be.

There's a lady in the Scriptures by the name of Naomi. Her name means "my joy." So when anyone said, "Hello, Naomi," they were saying, "Hello, my joy." "Good morning, Naomi. Good morning, my joy."

In Scripture, Naomi goes through a series of losses. Her husband dies. She becomes distraught. Then her sons are killed in battle. All these negative things hit her, and then she makes the mistake of letting the bitterness get on the inside. She gets soured on life. Her attitude is: *All my dreams have been shattered. Just leave me in my heartache and misery.*

But that's not God's plan. Sure, it's difficult when we go through a time of loss. There's a proper time for grieving. But we can't let a season of mourning turn into a lifetime of mourning. Naomi became so bitter she actually changed her name to Mara. Mara means "sorrow."

She had lost her joy and hope, so she asked to be called by the new name. Every time someone called her Mara, they were simply reminding her of her heartache and pain, and that made her feel even more defeated.

Don't let bad breaks change your meaning and purpose. You may have been through unfair situations. Maybe one of your dreams has died. Let me assure you God still has a great plan for your life. When one door closes, He will always open up another. You need to dig in your heels and say, "I may have been through a lot, but I've come too far to stop now. I refuse to get bitter. I refuse to live my life in the negative. I know God has great things in store."

David said in Psalm 27:13: "What would have become of me had I not believed to see the Lord's goodness." No matter what comes your way, let this take root. You have to believe you will see God's goodness again. You must believe you will see God turn it around. Believe you will see God open up new doors.

When you feel like dying, you should talk about living. When you feel like giving up, you should talk about pressing forward. When you don't see any way out, you must talk about how God can make a way. And know this: The enemy always fights you the hardest when he knows God has something great in store.

When the bottom falls out and it looks like you hit an all-time low . . . when it just couldn't get any worse . . . you don't know what God has around the corner. That is not the time to get bitter. That's not the time to get negative. That is the time to put your shoulders back and boldly declare: "My time is coming. I am a victor and not a victim."

Maybe you are like Naomi; you feel your life's been put on hold. You've had so much go against you and so many things have not worked. Negative thoughts are telling you: *It never will change. It never will be better. You never will be healthy. You never will be happy.*

Don't believe the "never" lies. God says, "Your time is coming."

CONSIDER THIS: Maybe you were counting on somebody to give you breaks. You were good to them. You went out of your way to help them succeed. But when you needed help, they were nowhere to be found.

Understand your destiny is not tied to them. Don't be discouraged because somebody walked away. Don't be bitter toward a boss, a business associate, a friend who was promoted and forgot all about you. You don't need them to succeed. God already has the right people lined up to come into your life. He has your divine connections.

I don't think of all the misery but of the beauty that still remains.

—*Anne Frank*

WHAT THE SCRIPTURES SAY

[What, what would have become of me] had I not believed that I
would see the Lord's goodness in the land of the living!

—Psalm 27:13 (AMP)

But now, Lord, what do I look for? My hope is in you.

—Psalm 39:7 (NIV)

A PRAYER FOR TODAY

Father, I've been through many challenges, but I've come too far
to stop now. I put my hope in You. Thank You for having great
things in store for me.

_____

_____

The greatest discovery of my
generation is that a human
being can alter his life by
altering his attitudes.

—William James

_____

_____

_____

_____

_____

_____

_____

TAKEAWAY TRUTH: Things are always darkest before the dawn. Have faith. Hold on to hope. God rewards those who wait.

DAY 7

KEEP YOUR FAITH STIRRED UP

KEY TRUTH: Even the worst can lead to good.

Thomas was alone on his boat when a big storm rose up. His boat capsized. He swam to shore and found himself alone on a deserted island. As the weeks passed, Thomas became so miserable, so distraught. He didn't think he would ever be found. He prayed and prayed, but the heavens seemed silent. Just when he thought it couldn't get any worse, his thatched-roof hut caught fire.

Thomas sat there weeping as his shelter went up in flames. It was like pouring salt on his wounds.

"God, I give up," he said. "I ask You to help me, but one bad thing after another happens."

He was so down, so discouraged.

Then, about an hour later, a Coast Guard rescue boat pulled up to the beach. Thomas could not believe it. He was thrilled.

"How in the world did you find me?" he asked.

"We saw the smoke coming from the signal fire you built," they said.

Sometimes what looks like a disappointment is simply God getting us in position for a rescue! You may feel defeated and beaten down today. But instead of being negative and bitter, why don't you take a different perspective? Believe that God will somehow, someway, turn the burning fires to your advantage.

Maybe you've been through disappointing relationships and you are feeling that time has passed you by. You're tempted to think that you are not meant to find the right person. No, God has already picked out the right person. And you're never too old. I know of one couple who met when both were in their nineties. That may not be your dream, but know that it's never too late for your time to come.

Maybe God's put a promise in your heart that one day you'll own a successful company or that you'll do mission work overseas. Don't give up on that promise. Don't give in to negative thoughts. Know that sometimes the more we believe, the more we pray, the less likely it looks. It's easy to get complacent and to let the seed die stillborn. But I'm asking you to hold on to that dream. Get up every morning and declare: "My time is coming. The promise is in me, and I will not die until I see it come to pass."

CONSIDER THIS: It's never too late. God says, "This is your season. Keep your faith stirred up." God never destroys a dream. We may give up on it. It may be delayed. But the seed God put in you never dies. My advice is to stay faithful. Your time is coming. God is keeping the records. He sees every seed you've ever sown. *What you sow you will reap.*

_____

_____

_____

_____

_____

—∞—

Everything that is done in
the world is done by hope.

—*Rev. Martin
Luther King, Jr.*

WHAT THE SCRIPTURES SAY

Why are you downcast, O my soul? Why so disturbed within
me? Put your hope in God, for I will yet praise him, my Savior
and my God.

—*Psalms 43:5 (NIV)*

Then the LORD answered me and said:
Write the vision
And make *it* plain on tablets
That he may run who reads it.
For the vision *is* yet for an appointed time;
But at the end it will speak, and it will not lie.
Though it tarries, wait for it;
Because it will surely come,
It will not tarry.
Behold the proud,
His soul is not upright in him;
But the just shall live by his faith.

—*Habakkuk 2:2–4 (NKJV)*

A PRAYER FOR TODAY

Father, my life is in the palm of Your hand. I don't know when better days will come, but I have faith in Your goodness and mercy. You know what is best for me. Help me to be patient while Your plan unfolds and until better days come.

Let me enjoy the earth no less
Because the all-enacting Might
That fashioned forth its loveliness
Had other aims than my delight.

—*Thomas Hardy*

TAKEAWAY TRUTH: I need to be in a position of faith so God can find me and put me where I need to be to fulfill His promise.

It's Time for Favor

"It's Time for Favor" is the section about faith fortification. Here you can bulk up with encouragement to pray bold prayers, to seek thriving over surviving, to choose faith over fear, to expect favor in your future, and to speak faith-filled words.

DAY 1

BE BOLD IN YOUR PRAYERS

KEY TRUTH: If you expect big and believe big, God will do big things in your life.

There are those who do ask for God's favor, but they pray such *small* prayers. "God, if You'll just give me a fifty-cent raise."

You'd better be careful with those small prayers. You might get what you ask for! Is that truly what you want?

"God, I've changed my mind. Give me that twenty-dollar raise instead! That's more like it!"

Other times you might say: "God, if You will just help my marriage survive." Or "God, just help me make ends meet this month." Or "God, help my child stay in school."

You must be bolder than that! Dare to pray: "God, I'm asking You not to just supply my needs but to bless me so much that I can be a blessing to others!"

Supersize your prayers:

"God, I'm asking that our marriage not just survive, but that we grow happier and more fulfilled than ever before!"

"God, I'm asking that my child become 'mighty in the land,' a leader and fulfilled of his God-given destiny!"

Jesus put it this way: "According to your faith it will be done unto you." That means if you pray for a little, you will receive a little. But if you can learn to pray bold prayers, and big prayers, and expect big, and believe big, God will do big things in your life.

The Scripture says in Psalm 2:8: "Ask of Me, and I surely will give the nations as Your inheritance."

God wants you to ask Him for big things. Ask Him for those hidden dreams planted in your heart. Ask Him even for the unborn promises that might otherwise never come to pass in the natural. Ask him to restore your broken ties to family members and other loved ones. Ask him for a life free of illness. Ask him for a full blossoming of your talents.

Do you ever feel like you are inconveniencing God? Are you content to just barely get by in life, to just endure it? Some people think they are being humble by not asking God for things, but Jesus paid a precious price to give us abundant life! He loves to hear us call upon His name!

I encourage you today: be bold and dare to believe God. Don't just think *survival* when God is thinking *abundance*. If you think bigger, you'll see God act bigger in your life. When you release your faith in a big way, God doesn't say, "Who do they think they are? The nerve of those people." No, when you stretch your faith, it brings a smile to God's face. He probably says to the angels, "Listen to what they're saying. They believe I can do great things. They believe I can turn any situation around. They've got their trust and confidence in Me, so I'm not going to disappoint them!"

It says in Hebrews: "So let us come boldly to the throne of our gracious God." The verse doesn't say, "Come to Me with a weak, defeated, pitiful attitude." He doesn't say, "Come to Me thinking about all your failures and how unworthy you are." No, God says, come to Me with boldness. Come to Me with your head held high, knowing that I'm a good God, and I want to help you! He says, "Come to Me knowing that you are the apple of My eye, and I want to be good to you."

And really, the only way you're going to approach God boldly is by knowing that you're righteous—that you are in right standing with Him. You have to know in your heart that God is pleased with you. You have to know that your sins are forgiven.

You may not be all that you're supposed to be yet, but you can thank God that you're not what you used to be! You are forgiven. You are chosen. You are accepted. Receive His forgiveness today so you can go boldly to His throne of grace.

CONSIDER THIS: The Scripture says that our faith pleases God, so take a step of faith today, and dare to believe that God will do the impossible in your life!

Boldness has genius, power, and magic in it. Begin it now.

—*Johann Wolfgang von Goethe*

WHAT THE SCRIPTURES SAY

> Ask of Me, and I will surely give the nations as Your inheritance,
> And the very ends of the earth as Your possession.
>
> —*Psalm 2:8 (NASB)*

> So let us come boldly to the throne of our gracious God. There
> we will receive his mercy, and we will find grace to help us when
> we need it most.
>
> —*Hebrews 4:16 (NLT)*

A PRAYER FOR TODAY

Father, thank You for Your mercy and grace. Thank You for inviting me into Your presence. I receive Your forgiveness today and come boldly before You. Teach me Your ways that I may walk in Your truth all the days of my life.

Be bold, be bold, and
everywhere be bold.

—*Herbert Spencer*

_____

_____

_____

_____

_____

_____

TAKEAWAY TRUTH: Jesus paid a precious price to give us abundant life, and He loves to hear us boldly call upon His name.

DAY 2

THE DARKER THE TIME,
THE BOLDER THE PRAYER

KEY TRUTH: Even in the darkest of moments you should dare to pray bold prayers.

Scripture says to ask and keep on asking. Knock and keep on knocking. If we have to ask for years, we should keep asking, keep believing, keep hoping on in faith.

Keep your faith flowing even when there is no hope in sight. Dare to dream big and pray boldly especially—yes, especially—when there is no hope in sight! If you don't believe me, believe Amber Wells. She is a frequent flyer and a frequent prayer. Amber has a ritual on every flight. As the airplane is taking off, Amber counts off the first 120 seconds. She read that once a plane has been in the air for two minutes after takeoff, most typical problems have been avoided.

But on a flight in early 2008, Amber had only made it to ninety seconds in her count when something went terribly wrong. She heard a loud explosion, and then, from her seat in the twentieth row, she saw a fireball come out of the plane's engine.

Amber then noticed that the pilot had begun to slowly turn the plane, as if heading back toward the airport. But then he said over the loudspeaker: "Brace for impact, brace for impact."

After that announcement, everyone around Amber began praying softly. She held on to the cross on her necklace, closed her eyes, and joined them.

Amber prayed: "Lord, guide the hand of this pilot. Let us be safe. Watch over us. Protect us."

The next thing she knew, she was knee-deep in water. She looked out the window and saw that her plane was no longer in the air. She was surrounded by water.

You know what happened from there. Amber Wells and everyone else on her US Airways Flight 1549 plane made it to safety. Amber told a reporter later that the 155 people who survived the emergency landing "are living proof of God's grace, because we wouldn't be here without Him." Those survivors offer impressive evidence that even in the darkest of moments you should dare to pray bold prayers. The only way you're going to be as bold as a lion is to know that you have been made righteous through Jesus. When you know who you are in Christ, when you know that God is smiling upon you and that your sins are forgiven, then you're going to hold your shoulders back and have the boldness and confidence that God really wants you to have.

Being righteous doesn't mean that you're perfect. It doesn't mean that you don't make mistakes. Righteousness is being in right standing with God. If you have accepted Jesus as your Lord and Savior and have a desire to please Him, then you have been made righteous. You have been born into God's very own family. You did not do anything to earn this righteousness; it's simply a gift. Receive His gift of righteousness today so you can move forward in the boldness and victory He has for you!

CONSIDER THIS: Because of Jesus' obedience in paying the price for our sin, we are made righteous through Him!

_____

_____

_____

_____

_____

_____   —❧—

_____

_____   The mind, ever the willing
servant, will respond to
_____   boldness, for boldness, in
effect, is a command to
_____   deliver mental resources.

_____   *—Norman Vincent Peale*

_____

_____

_____

_____

_____

_____

WHAT THE SCRIPTURES SAY

The wicked man flees though no one pursues,
but the righteous are as bold as a lion.
—Proverbs 28:1 (NIV)

For as by one man's disobedience many were made sinners, so
also by one Man's obedience many will be made righteous.
—Romans 5:19 (NKJV)

A PRAYER FOR TODAY

Father, thank You for sending Your Son to pay the penalty for my sin. As a believer in Jesus, I receive Your righteousness by faith today so that I can live in boldness and confidence all the days of my life.

_____

_____

_____

_____

_____

_____

℞

We make way for the man
who boldly pushes past us.

—*Christian Nevell Bovee*

_____

_____

_____

_____

_____

_____

TAKEAWAY TRUTH: If you have accepted Jesus as your Lord and Savior and have a desire to please Him, then you have been made righteous.

DAY 3

EXPECT THE BEST

KEY TRUTH: A survival mentality will keep you from God's best.

A young lady once told me she divorced her husband after years of struggling in their marriage. She had done her best to keep it together, but it just didn't work out.

"At least now I'm surviving," she said.

She was happy that she made it through, but I could tell the wind was out of her sails. This beautiful girl had lost the sparkle in her eyes. I told her it was good that she'd put the bad marriage behind her, but I added, "Now, you must leave that survival mentality behind you, too. God has new seasons in front of you. He has new doors He wants to open. He wants the next part of your life to be better than the first part. But you can't make the mistake of just settling and thinking: *I've been through so much. I'm just glad to be where I am.*"

A survival mentality will keep you from God's best. You must shake it off. Pray for God's help: *You promised that what was meant for my harm You would use to my advantage. I may have been through the fire, through the famine, through the flood, but I know it's my time for favor. It's my time to see more of Your goodness in my life.*

Make up your mind that no matter what comes your way, no matter how difficult, no matter how unfair, you will do more than simply survive. You will thrive in spite of it. There are things beyond our control, but not God's control. In one sense, it doesn't really matter what the stock market does or doesn't do. It doesn't matter how high the price of gas goes. God always has the final say. If hard times hit, God can still bless you in a greater way.

"I have not seen the righteous forsaken, nor his seed begging bread," David says in the Psalms. And Matthew 6:33 promises that if you seek first the kingdom of God and His righteousness, all essential things "shall be added unto you."

Still, sometimes we get talked into thinking like survivors. We see so many negative news reports we begin to worry: *It's so bad. How will I make it?*

No. I want to talk you into thriving and not just surviving. I realize we need to be wise and use the wisdom God has given us, but I don't believe you are supposed to pull back and not pursue your dreams, not expect increase, not believe in favor, or just try to hold on. That is a survival mentality.

Times may become difficult. You may wonder how things will work out. But remember this: As God took the five loaves and the two fish and multiplied them to feed thousands of people, He can multiply what you have.

God can multiply your time and help you to get more done. He can multiply your wisdom and help you make better decisions. He can multiply your finances so your money goes further. God is in complete control.

When tough times hit, don't hunker down and think: *Oh, it's so bad. I just have to hold on and try to make it through.* No, dig in your heels and say: "I will not just survive. I will thrive. I will prosper in spite of this difficulty."

CONSIDER THIS: People get confused sometimes and think they have to go chasing after the blessings. But really, when you chase after God each and every day, when you make Him your highest priority, the blessings will automatically follow. Today, make pleasing the Lord first on your list. Let go of any weights or sins that you know are holding you back. Be willing to deal with any issues God brings to light. Don't give in to compromise and temptation because all that will do is keep you from God's best. Instead, make the decision to daily put Him first and keep your heart pure before Him. Then get ready because His blessings will chase you down as He daily loads you with benefits!

It takes but one positive thought when given a chance to survive and thrive to overpower an entire army of negative thoughts.

—Robert H. Schuller

WHAT THE SCRIPTURES SAY

> Blessed *be* the Lord,
> *Who* daily loads us *with benefits.*
> —*Psalm 68:19 (NKJV)*

But seek first His kingdom and His righteousness, and all these things will be added to you.

—*Matthew 6:33 (NASB)*

A PRAYER FOR TODAY

Father God, today I dedicate every area of my life to You. Help me to live a life of integrity and honor. Thank You for daily loading me with benefits as I put You first in everything that I do.

_____

_____

_____

To accomplish great things, we must not only act but also dream, not only plan but also believe.

—*Anatole France*

_____

_____

_____

_____

_____

_____

_____

_____

TAKEAWAY TRUTH: God can multiply what I have.

DAY 4

ACCEPT NO LIMITS

KEY TRUTH: God is only limited by our thinking.

My sister Lisa and her husband Kevin found a new house that met their needs, so they decided to sell theirs. Most homes in their neighborhood were taking three months to a year to sell. They prayed and asked God for His help. On the first day their house went on the market, a woman called and said she wanted to buy it. Not only that, she said, "If you'll take it off the market right now, I'll pay you more than you have it listed for."

That is unprecedented favor. A bad economy does not limit God's power. What goes on around us does not limit Him. God is only limited by our thinking. That is why it is so important that we don't fall into survival mode and start thinking, *My business can't expand. The economy is too slow. I'll never sell my house because no others are selling. I'll never get a promotion when the business is cutting back.*

God likes to show up and show out in hard times. He likes to do the extraordinary because it brings Him more honor. When we spread the good news of what God has done—*I had my best year in a bad year. I sold my house when no others were selling. My crops survived the killing frost*—our words honor God.

Get ready for God to show up and show out in your life in a

greater way. God wants to do the extraordinary. He wants to make you an example of his goodness.

If you believe to barely get by, you will barely get by.

If you believe that you will have a tough year, your faith will draw that in. So I encourage you to believe that you are blessed— not that you will be blessed—but that you are already blessed. Believe God's favor surrounds you in a greater way.

You may say: "Joel, I don't really feel blessed. I don't feel like I have favor. I never get any good breaks." This is what faith is all about. You must believe it before you see it. You need to act like you're blessed, talk like you're blessed, think like you're blessed, dress like you're blessed, walk like you're blessed, treat people like you're blessed.

That's your faith at work. You will draw in the goodness and favor of God. And that's a whole lot better than fretting that the value of your home dropped $10,000 overnight, or that your company is downsizing, or that the price of groceries has gone through the roof.

CONSIDER THIS: We all have opportunities to lose our joy and get discouraged trying to endure life. But God never intended for us to just endure life. He created us to enjoy life. And whether you realize it or not, you prepare for either victory or defeat at the start of every day. When you get up in the morning, you have to choose to set your mind in the right direction. You may feel discouraged. You may be thinking, *I don't want to go to work today. I don't want to deal with these children. I've got so many problems.* However, if you dwell on those negative thoughts, then you are preparing for a lousy day. Instead, turn it around and say, "This is going to be a great day. Something good is going to happen to me. God has favor in my future, and I'm expecting new opportunities, divine connections, and supernatural breakthroughs." When you take on this attitude, you are preparing for victory, increase, and restoration! Having an attitude of faith allows God to show up and show out in unusual ways. It opens the door for Him to work in your life and pour out His supernatural blessing on you!

_____

_____

_____

_____

_____

_____   —❦—————

_____   I myself do nothing. The

_____   Holy Spirit accomplishes

     all through me.

_____

     —William Blake

_____

_____

_____

_____

_____

_____

_____

_____

_____

_____

WHAT THE SCRIPTURES SAY

Now set your mind and heart to seek (inquire of and require as your vital necessity) the Lord your God.

—*I Chronicles 22:19 (AMP)*

This is my command—be strong and courageous! Do not be afraid or discouraged. For the LORD your God is with you wherever you go.

—*Joshua 1:9 (NLT)*

A PRAYER FOR TODAY

Father in heaven, I choose to set my heart and mind on You today. I know that You have good things planned for me. Use me to be a blessing to others.

———————————————

———————————————

———— ✥ ————

The human spirit fails, except when the Holy Spirit fills.

—*Corrie ten Boom*

_____

_____

_____

_____

_____

_____

_____

_____

TAKEAWAY TRUTH: God likes to show up and show out in hard times.

DAY 5

FOCUS ON SOLUTIONS, NOT PROBLEMS

KEY TRUTH: As a child of the Most High God, as long as you are walking in His ways, you have the blessing of God on your life

Psychologists and researchers who study "hope theory" have found that focusing on solutions increases our capacity to reach our goals while lifting our spirits in the process.

I met a couple who had lost everything in Hurricane Katrina. They moved to Houston and found temporary housing. When I spoke with them, I could tell they were still in survival mode. They could not see beyond their temporary situation to a new and better life. They were just grateful to be making it though another day, another month. I felt a need to jump-start their faith. I reminded them that God has promised to pay back double for every unfair thing that happens to us.

God said He would make us better off than we were before, but first we have to shake off the survival mentality. Get in agreement with God. Focus forward and say: "It's payback time. I know my God is a God of restoration, and I believe it's my time for favor. I may be in the desert right now, but I know God can prosper me even there. I know if God is for me, who would dare be against me?"

Understand that as a child of the Most High God, as long as you are walking in His ways, you have the blessing of God on your life. Wherever you go, His blessings go. You can be out in the desert and God will cause you to be blessed. You can be working at an office with negative people, with people who complain constantly, but when you get there, the blessing gets there. Really, your company should be glad to have you because you bring the blessing. You bring God's favor.

In the Scripture, we are told that when Job prayed for his friends, the Lord gave him twice as much as he'd had before. God gave him an "I-told-you-so" moment!

Don't dwell on your problems. If you have a poor mouth, you will have a poor life. Your life may be full of challenges, but you are still connected to the Vine. Your dreams and plans may seem to be falling apart, but God is still on the throne. You may not see a way out because your resources are limited, but God owns it all. Stay in faith. Make the decision that you will thrive, not merely survive.

So many people today are living with less than God's best because they've allowed fear to stop them from pursuing their dreams. We have to remember that fear is not from God. It's a lie from the enemy to paralyze us and steal our power.

God has given us power, love, and self-discipline or self-control. When you are confident in God's promises, there's nothing that can stop you. But when fear creeps in, you hesitate. You're not as strong as you were before. You feel powerless. Not only that, but it affects your love. Love prompts us to give, and when we are afraid, we tend to clench our fists and act selfishly. Fear also affects our self-discipline. It makes us panic and do things without thinking.

CONSIDER THIS: If you've allowed fear to steal from you in any area of life, today you can be free—you can be finished with fear. As you step out and away from fear, God will be with you. He'll give you power, love, and self-discipline so that you can confidently move forward into the abundant life He has for you!

The ultimate measure of a man is not where he stands in moments of comfort and convenience, but where he stands at times of challenge and controversy.

—*Rev. Martin Luther King, Jr.*

WHAT THE SCRIPTURES SAY

When Job prayed for his friends, the LORD restored his fortunes. In fact, the LORD gave him twice as much as before.

—Job 42:10 (NLT)

For God has not given us a spirit of fear and timidity, but of power, love, and self-discipline.

—2 Timothy 1:7 (NLT)

A PRAYER FOR TODAY

Father God, I come to You today declaring that I am determined to thrive. I am finished with fear. Thank You for giving me power, love, and a sound mind. I choose to stand on Your promises. Fill me with Your peace and joy today as I move forward in victory with You.

My mission in life is not merely to survive, but to thrive; and to do so with some passion, some compassion, some humor, and some style.

—Maya Angelou

_____

_____

_____

_____

_____

_____

_____

_____

_____

_____

TAKEAWAY TRUTH: Conquering fear starts with a choice to believe God's promises and then taking a step of faith to act on them.

DAY 6

KEEP GOD FIRST

KEY TRUTH: People of faith are continually in bloom.

Recently, one of our church members told me he'd encountered some rough going. Then he said, "But Joel, I'm too blessed to be stressed." I like that. That's the way we need to be. "I'm too blessed to be worried. I'm too blessed to be negative. I'm too blessed to be upset. I've seen God do too many great things."

Psalm 1:3 says if we keep God first, we'll be like a tree planted by the waters. Our leaves will not wither. The Message translation says: "You're a tree replanted in Eden . . . always in blossom." I believe you are such a person. I believe people of faith are continually in bloom. People who smile when they could be complaining. People who sing a song of praise even when times are tough. Deep down you know that everywhere you go, you are blessed by God.

Now, you may have been in the survival mode for a long, long time. If you will get in agreement with God, I'll just declare that your days of survival are over and your days of thriving have begun. I want you to go in faith knowing that God has great things in your future.

A friend e-mailed me this story, about a twenty-three-year-old woman who supposedly had a wild experience after going to the grocery store. She returned to her car and put the groceries in the backseat. Then, just as she sat down behind the wheel, she heard a loud noise and felt something hit the back of her head. She thought she had been shot.

She reached up and felt what she thought were her brains coming out. She was so shocked, she passed out. Minutes later, she woke up, but still she was afraid to move. She sat there motionless for over an hour, holding the back of her head because she was afraid of losing more brain tissue.

Finally, a gentleman walked by and noticed that something was wrong. He called the police. The patrol officers showed up and asked her to open the car door. She said she couldn't. She said she'd been shot and she was holding her brains in.

The police broke open the window and discovered a pressurized can of Pillsbury biscuits had exploded. That dough had hit the back of her head. She'd felt it and thought her life was ending. When fear and worry dominate our thoughts, our minds can make the most innocent things seem threatening. So even if the economy is bad, or even if you are going through difficult times with your health or relationships, don't let negative thoughts blind you to reality.

CONSIDER THIS: Make the decision that you're not pulling back, hunkering down, or just holding on. Dig your heels in and say, "I am not just surviving. This is my year to thrive." If you'll do this, God will amaze you with His goodness. You will be a person who is always in bloom.

_____

_____

_____

_____

_____

_____

_____ ———— ✦ ————

_____ I can see, and that is why I

_____ can be happy, in what you call

_____ the dark, but which to me is

_____ golden. I can see a God-made

_____ world, not a man-made world.

_____ —*Helen Keller*

_____

_____

_____

WHAT THE SCRIPTURES SAY

Instead you thrill to GOD's Word,
you chew on Scripture day and night.
You're a tree replanted in Eden,
bearing fresh fruit every month,
never dropping a leaf,
always in blossom.

—*Psalm 1:3 (MSG)*

David was greatly distressed because the men were talking of
stoning him; each one was bitter in spirit because of his sons and
daughters. But David found strength in the LORD his God.

—*1 Samuel 30:6 (NIV)*

A PRAYER FOR TODAY

Father in heaven, thank You for giving me life. I choose today to agree with Your word, which says I can thrive and enjoy my life to the full. Help me see Your hand at work more and more each day. I thank You and give You praise.

A positive attitude may not solve all your problems, but it will annoy enough people to make it worth the effort.

—*Herm Albright*

TAKEAWAY TRUTH: When you live a life that honors God, when you obey His word and are a person of excellence and integrity, the Scripture says that God's blessings will chase you down and overtake you. You won't be able to outrun the good things of God. He daily loads us with benefits!

DAY 7

FOCUS ON FAITH, NOT FEAR

KEY TRUTH: When you dwell on your fears, you use your faith in reverse.

We have so many opportunities to be fearful in these times. People are concerned about the economy, worried about their health, fearful for their children. But God says to you what He said to me: "Don't use your energy to worry. Use your energy to believe."

Do you know that it takes the same amount of energy to believe as it does to worry? It's just as easy to say, "God is supplying all of my needs," as it is to say, "I will never make it."

It takes the same amount of effort to say, "I will live a long healthy life," as it does to say, "I don't think I'll ever get well."

When someone expresses fear about being laid off, I understand the concern. Your fears may be valid, too, but you can't go around meditating on them, expecting the worst, expecting to have a bad year.

When you dwell on your fears, you use your faith in reverse. Instead of constantly worrying, simply say, "God, my life is in Your hands. I know You're guiding and directing my steps, and I'm not expecting defeat. I'm not expecting failure. I'm expecting to have a blessed year. I'm expecting to go over and not under."

You might ask, "Joel, what if I do that and it doesn't happen?"

What if you do it and it does happen? Even if you were to get laid off, you don't have to get discouraged or think, *I knew it wouldn't work for me.*

Instead, stay in faith. Know that when one door closes, God will open up another. If you keep the right attitude, He'll give you a better job, with better benefits, making better money!

Faith opens the door for God to work in our lives. Fear opens the door for the enemy to work in our lives. Are you standing firm against the enemy today? When fear comes against you, do you dwell on those defeating thoughts or do you rise up and start confessing the promises of God over your life? If you choose to dwell on your fears and think about all the reasons why you can't do what God is telling you to, then before long you're going to develop a negative mindset that will hold you back. It's much more difficult to overcome than fear.

Don't allow the enemy to hold you back with fear any longer. Focus on that vision of victory. Be bold and step out in faith! Today is a new day! It's your new beginning. Just because you feel fear, doesn't mean you have to follow fear. Every person feels fear at some point. The greatest men and women of the Bible all felt fear. But when fear comes, don't give in! Stay the course of faith and follow God's word. Break that negative power over your life, and move forward into the freedom and joy He has in store for you!

The Bible says that fear has torment. Fear has no mercy. If you act on fear instead of acting on faith, it will keep you depressed, miserable, and lonely. And so many people today are missing out on God's joy, peace, and victory because they keep giving in to fear. They feed fear with what they watch on TV or at the movies. Don't let that be you! Scripture tells us that faith comes by hearing the word of God. The more you fill your heart and mind with God's word, the stronger you will be to stand against the powers of darkness. Choose faith instead of fear by choosing God's word.

CONSIDER THIS: You have the power to choose your response to fears. When thoughts come that say, "You're not able," choose faith by saying, "I can do all things through Christ!" Choose faith today so you can overcome fear and live in the freedom God has in store for you!

He has not learned the lesson of life who does not every day surmount a fear.

—*Ralph Waldo Emerson*

WHAT THE SCRIPTURES SAY

Consequently, faith comes from hearing the message, and the message is heard through the word of Christ.

—Romans 10:17 (NIV)

There is no fear in love; but perfect love casts out fear, because fear involves torment. But he who fears has not been made perfect in love.

—1 John 4:18 (NKJV)

A PRAYER FOR TODAY

Father, today I receive Your word, which is life, health, and strength to me. I choose to close the door on fear by guarding what I say, what I listen to, and what I dwell on. Help me guard my mouth today and speak words of faith.

_____

_____

_____

_____

_____

Those who fear life are already three parts dead.

—Bertrand Russell

_____

_____

_____

TAKEAWAY TRUTH: The power of God is greater than the power of fear.

It's Time for Restoration

In this section, you'll find the tools of forgiveness and renewal. These include God's ability to turn back time and your power to come back from setbacks and to bounce back from disappointments. Restoration comes, too, from living a resurrected life and from holding on to your promise of a better day.

DAY 1

NEVER SETTLE FOR LESS
THAN GOD'S BEST

KEY TRUTH: God can reset the clock in your life.

In the story of Hezekiah, God granted the sick man fifteen extra years of life. Naturally, Hezekiah was very excited when he got the news about his new lease on life. It was almost too good to be true. Just for peace of mind, he asked God for a sign.

Since they were dealing with time, God said, "Alright, Hezekiah. Go out and watch the sundial."

They didn't have clocks or wristwatches like we have today. They had markings on the ground to help them tell time according to the positions of the sun's shadows. That didn't stop Hezekiah from making a bold request. Basically, Hezekiah said, "God, if this promise is to come to pass, if You add years to my life, don't just stop time. I know You can do that. I want You to do something more difficult—something even more out of the ordinary. God, I'm asking You to make the shadow go in the wrong direction. I'm asking You to turn back time."

That took a lot of nerve. Hezekiah was putting God's love to the test by asking Him to do something that, as far as we know, God had never done before. He asked God to interrupt the entire solar system just to assure Hezekiah that His promise was sincere.

Sure enough, over the next forty minutes, Hezekiah watched the shadow go counterclockwise. The Scripture says that the sun went in reverse ten degrees. God was sending us a message. I believe He was saying, "I can reset the clock in your life. I can restore the years you've lost."

Every one has regretted missing opportunities at some point. They've wondered why they didn't put more effort into a job or a relationship or a business opportunity. I once had a man tell me that he couldn't believe that he was ever going to come into a new season of increase because he'd missed his season. I assured him that God always has another season. He is a God of restoration. Another chance is always awaiting those in faith.

Circumstances beyond our control can force us to miss out. Some people don't have the opportunities because they've grown up in poverty, in a broken family, or even worse conditions. They may be tempted to think that they'll never have a chance at a better life. That's not true. God can make up for the lost years.

You may not be able to go back in time, but you can go forward in faith. Don't be discouraged. Believe that for every missed opportunity, there is a better one awaiting you. For every door closed by hard times, another can be reopened by God's hand.

If you feel joys and blessings have been stolen away from you, know that God wants to give you back twice as much as you've lost. Twice as much joy. Twice as much peace. Twice as much fulfillment in your relationships, your job, or your charitable work. What's happened in the past has passed. Choose to release those memories by forgiving those who've hurt you. Open your heart, and invite the God of restoration to write a new and better chapter in your life. Let Him give you a fresh start that is better than anything you might have imagined.

CONSIDER THIS: We serve a God of restoration! You may have had some disappointments or unfair things happen in your life; but instead of dwelling on the past and living in defeat, choose to focus on His promises because God wants to restore everything that's been stolen from your life. He wants to restore your joy, your peace, your health, and your finances. But here's the key: You have to have a vision of it. You have to get your hopes up and decide to get your thoughts and words going in the right direction. Today, choose to focus on the future and release past hurts through forgiveness. Draw a line in the sand and say, "I am a child of the Most High God, and I'm not going to live my life negative and defeated. This is a new day, and I'm taking back what belongs to me!" That's having a restoration mentality!

_____

_____

_____   —————— ❧ ——————

_____

_____   Opportunity often

_____   comes disguised in the

_____   form of misfortune, or

_____   temporary defeat.

_____   *—Napoleon Hill*

_____   _____

_____

_____

_____

_____

_____

WHAT THE SCRIPTURES SAY

Hezekiah had asked Isaiah, "What will be the sign that the LORD will heal me and that I will go up to the temple of the LORD on the third day from now?"

Isaiah answered, "This is the LORD's sign to you that the LORD will do what he has promised: Shall the shadow go forward ten steps, or shall it go back ten steps?"

"It is a simple matter for the shadow to go forward ten steps," said Hezekiah. "Rather, have it go back ten steps."

Then the prophet Isaiah called upon the LORD, and the LORD made the shadow go back the ten steps it had gone down on the stairway of Ahaz.

—2 Kings 20:8–11 (NIV)

The Lord says, "I will give you back what you lost to the swarming locusts, the hopping locusts, the stripping locusts, and the cutting locusts. It was I who sent this great destroying army against you."

—Joel 2:25 (NLT)

A PRAYER FOR TODAY

Father, thank You for choosing to restore my life. Thank You for the truth of Your word that sets me free. Fill me with Your power today so that I may stand strong and move forward on the path You have for me. I love You and bless Your name.

_____

_____

_____

_____

_____

_____   ~⚬~

_____

_____   Become a possibilitarian.

_____   No matter how dark things
seem to be or actually are,

_____   raise your sights and see

_____   possibilities—always see them
for they're always there.

_____

                             —Norman Vincent Peale

_____

_____

_____

_____

TAKEAWAY TRUTH: You may not be able to go back in time, but you can go forward in faith.

DAY 2

STAY UPRIGHT
AGAINST CHALLENGES

KEY TRUTH: God rewards those who refuse to give up.

Gregory, a businessman, went through a legal battle for three and a half years. It was a challenging time. Some business competitors stirred up trouble. They made untrue allegations, and he had to defend himself. At first he was strong and determined. Gregory did his best to fight the good fight. But as the charges and countercharges dragged on month after month, he eventually lost his joy for the business. He was run-down, just tired of fighting.

As it dragged on, Gregory made a sad statement one day.

"Joel, I don't really care anymore," he said. "This thing has about ruined me. It's about ruined my business. I don't think it will ever change."

It's very unhealthy to have an "I don't care" attitude. That's when people can make major mistakes and do things they regret later on. I told Gregory that God wants to restore those years he's lost fighting the competition in court. He may not see how it can happen, but God is a supernatural God.

If you'll stay in faith, God will not only bring you out; He'll also turn back time. God will make up for the lost joy. He'll make up for the lost peace. He'll restore your victories.

That's exactly what happened to Gregory. Several years after he told me that he'd lost his joy in the business his legal problems came to a successful end. God vindicated him. Today he's stronger, happier, more blessed than he's ever been.

Maybe, like Gregory, you are in a difficult situation. It's been dragging on and dragging your spirits down in the process. Maybe your struggle has stolen your joy, stolen your peace. Let me encourage you. You've got to stand strong and stay positive. Declare your determination by faith: "This thing will not defeat me. I may have lost years, but I know God will restore these years. He will bring me out. He will leave me better off than I was before."

Did you know that all of your days have already been written? God has already recorded every part of your life from the beginning to the end. He knows every disappointment, every loss, and every challenge. The good news is that even though you've had some challenges, even though you've faced some setbacks, your story ends in victory. Your final chapter concludes with you fulfilling your God-given destiny and experiencing His eternal restoration.

Any time we face a disappointment in life or go through a loss, we have to remember there's another chapter in front of us. We can't give up; we have to keep moving forward. Instead of focusing on what didn't work out, wondering why we went through a marriage that didn't last, or why we didn't get that position we worked so hard for, we must focus on the future. Let go of the past and press forward, because your story ends in victory, and God will restore everything that has been stolen from you!

CONSIDER THIS: You are a three-part being: You have a spirit—that's the part of you that lives for eternity—you have a soul, and you have your body while you're here on earth. Your soul is where the enemy tries to wound you and hold you back. Your soul is where you may have brokenness from the past or hurts and disappointments. When God restores your soul, He brings His healing power to those broken places. He makes you whole again. And when God restores you, He makes you better off than you were before! When we are resting in Him, He is able to do a work in our lives. He is able to bring that restoration. Don't let a busy life keep you going so fast that you never stop and rest. Take time to be still before the Lord and meditate on His word. As you do, He will restore and heal your soul, and you will live the life of victory God has planned for you!

Start by doing what's necessary; then do what's possible; and suddenly you are doing the impossible.

—*St. Francis of Assisi*

WHAT THE SCRIPTURES SAY

> The LORD *is* my shepherd;
> I shall not want.
> He makes me to lie down in green pastures;
> He leads me beside the still waters.
> He restores my soul;
> He leads me in the paths of righteousness
> For His name's sake.
>
> *—Psalm 23:1–3 (NKJV)*

> For the LORD God *is* a sun and shield;
> The LORD will give grace and glory;
> No good *thing* will He withhold
> From those who walk uprightly.
>
> *—Psalm 84:11 (NKJV)*

A PRAYER FOR TODAY

Heavenly Father, thank You for setting me up for victory. Thank You for holding me in the palm of Your hand. I choose to release the questions and disappointments in the past so that I can receive the victory You have prepared for me!

_____

_____

_____

_____

_____

_____

_____

_____

_____   ⧽⧼

_____

_____   Most of the important
                              things in the world have
_____   been accomplished by
                              people who have kept on
_____   trying when there seemed
                              to be no hope at all.
_____
                              —*Dale Carnegie*
_____

_____

_____

_____

TAKEAWAY TRUTH: When God restores your soul, He brings
His healing power to those broken places. He makes you whole
again.

DAY 3

YOU HAVE COMEBACK POWER

KEY TRUTH: You may feel buried by disappointments, but instead you've been planted to rise and grow anew.

John was among the thousands of reporters and editors faced with layoffs in the newspaper industry. Even before the recession hit, newspapers were hurting because advertisers and readers were shifting to the internet. When the economy sank, the newspaper business went down faster than anyone expected.

With a daughter in college and another in grade school, John had to keep working. So he transferred from the newspaper's print news team where jobs were disappearing to its growing website team. Over the next six months, he learned how to create and manage a digital news website. It was a challenge mastering the new technology. But John felt he had to adapt.

When the next round of layoffs hit his newspaper, more than one hundred people lost their jobs. John was one of the few who quit on his own terms. You see, while others were swept up by bad events, John stepped up, took control, and rose above his circumstances.

Instead of mourning that his career was dead and buried, he grabbed the shovel and planted the seeds of a new one. Many of his former coworkers went on unemployment. They struggled to make ends meet. But John took his new website skills just a few miles up the road to a local television station. There, he began a new career as the television station's digital media manager, for an even better salary.

At some point, we all face major challenges—the loss of a job, a broken relationship, an illness—that easily could bury us in despair. Negative thoughts can overpower you at such times, bombarding your mind, telling you, *It's over. You've seen your best days. Your future is tainted. Your life is ruined.*

Yet there is a difference between being buried and being planted. That difference boils down to your expectation of what happens next. When you put a seed in the ground, you don't say, "I'm burying this seed." You say, "I'm planting this seed."

The difference is that when you plant a seed, you expect to see it rise again and come back to life.

Now, there is a time and a place for both burying and planting. Not long ago one of our pet rabbits died. I didn't say, "I'm planting this rabbit." I buried that rabbit. I knew it wasn't coming back. If it did, I sure didn't want to be around.

CONSIDER THIS: When you go through disappointments and you're in tough times, you may feel like you've been buried, but the fact is you've simply been planted. That means you're coming back. And you're not only coming back, you will come back better, increased, stronger.

You go in as a seed, but because of the life of God, you come out blossomed, producing even more fruit.

_____

_____

_____

_____

_____

_____

_____   ❧

_____   Not knowing when the Dawn
                                            will come,
_____   I open every Door.

_____   —*Emily Dickinson*

_____

_____

_____

_____

_____

WHAT THE SCRIPTURES SAY

I tell you the truth, unless a kernel of wheat is planted in the soil
and dies, it remains alone. But its death will produce many new
kernels—a plentiful harvest of new lives. Those who love their
life in this world will lose it. Those who care nothing for their
life in this world will keep it for eternity. Anyone who wants
to be my disciple must follow me, because my servants must be
where I am. And the Father will honor anyone who serves me.

—*John 12:24 (NLT)*

For though a righteous man falls seven times, he rises again.

—*Proverbs 24:16a (NIV)*

A PRAYER FOR TODAY

Father, thank You for setting me up for success in everything I do. I choose to trust and rely on You knowing that Your plans are for my good. Help me to look ahead in faith and with expectancy.

Nothing is hopeless; we must hope for everything.

—*Madeleine L'Engle*

TAKEAWAY TRUTH: Remember, as a believer, the same power that raised Christ from the dead lives on the inside of you. There is no challenge too difficult, no obstacle too high, no sickness, no disappointment, no person, nothing that can keep you from your God-given destiny. If you stay in faith and keep a good attitude, you will rise again. God will turn those stumbling blocks into stepping-stones, and you'll move forward into the victory He has in store for you!

DAY 4

YOU CAN RISE AGAIN
AND FLOURISH

KEY TRUTH: What was meant for your harm, God will use to your advantage.

In John 12:24, Jesus said the time for planting comes when challenges arise. We all face difficulties, but you have the seed of Almighty God on the inside. He breathed His life into you. Jesus talked about this in John 12:24. He said that unless a grain of wheat falls into the ground and is planted, it will not produce fruit. You can have a seed lying on the shelf for a lifetime, but it will never become what it was created to be until you put it in the ground.

The seed's potential will never be fully realized until it's planted. As long as it's up on the shelf where it's comfortable, where it doesn't have to stretch and doesn't have to deal with any adversities, that potential will remain dormant. Only after it's been planted and it goes through the process of germination—the outer shield breaks off, the new growth springs forth—will it blossom and produce more fruit.

Being planted isn't a comfortable experience. It's dark down there. But when you are planted, you know you will rise to the light. Something supernatural starts to happen. Although the earth is heavy, it cannot hold the seed in. I can imagine you, the seed, rising defiantly through the soil with the conviction that you have the life of God within you.

Sure enough, one day that little seed breaks the surface of the earth. No longer buried, it rises and grows stronger than ever before. It's a new beginning with even greater potential to be realized.

You can store a seed on the shelf for a lifetime. It will never become what it was created to be until you put the seed in the ground so that it can fulfill its potential. As long as the seed is on the shelf, it may be comfortable, but it is dormant. The same holds true with people facing hard times. You can stay on the shelf. You don't have to stretch. You don't have to deal with adversity. In the meantime, your potential will remain locked up on the inside.

As time goes by, instead of being a little seed buried in the ground, your seed grows into a beautiful plant producing bright, colorful flowers. What happened? The seed had to go through some dark times, some lonely nights. It had to push tons of dirt out of the way. Sometimes, the seed felt that it would never see bright days, but it pressed forward. Eventually, as God intended, His creation burst through the darkness into the light, grew, and flourished.

No matter what comes against you in life, you are not buried. You are planted. You may feel as though you are buried in dirt right now. You're in a tough time. Something was unfair. It seems like your situation will never change.

But if you keep shaking off the self-pity, shaking off the negative thoughts, then you, too—like that little seed—will begin to feel the life of God spring forth. The same power that raised Christ from the dead is on the inside of you. That sickness will tell you: "You can't push me out of the way. I'm much bigger than you. I've got you buried." Don't believe that lie.

Just say, "I'm coming back. This economy may have knocked me down. It may have cost me my job. It may have drained my savings. But I'm not buried. I'm planted. I've got comeback power. This is not the end. It's only the beginning." Or in a different scenario: "I may be lying in the hospital right now, but this sickness is only temporary. This chemo may have taken my strength, my energy, my hair. But know this today: I've got comeback power. This is not the end. It's only the beginning."

CONSIDER THIS: When you have faith, your potential is never buried. Know that whomever the Son sets free is free indeed. God has another victory in your future.

I am responsible. Although I may not be able to prevent the worst from happening, I am responsible for my attitude toward the inevitable misfortunes that darken life. Bad things do happen; how I respond to them defines my character and the quality of my life. I can choose to sit in perpetual sadness, immobilized by the gravity of my loss, or I can choose to rise from the pain and treasure the most precious gift I have—life itself.

—*Walter Anderson*

_____

_____

_____

_____

_____

_____

_____

WHAT THE SCRIPTURES SAY

Why are you downcast, O my soul? Why so disturbed within me? Put your hope in God, for I will yet praise him, my Savior and my God.

—Psalm 42:5–6a (NIV)

Jesus said unto her, I am the resurrection, and the life: he that believeth in me, though he were dead, yet shall he live.

—John 11:25 (KJV)

A PRAYER FOR TODAY

Father, thank You for giving me strength to overcome every obstacle in life. I choose to rejoice no matter what may come against me because I know You are working all things together for my good. Thank You for developing Your character in me.

_____

_____

_____

_____

_____

You may encounter many
defeats, but you must not
be defeated. In fact, it may
be necessary to encounter
the defeats so you can
know who you are, what
you can rise from, how you
can still come out of it.

—*Maya Angelou*

TAKEAWAY TRUTH: When the worst happens to you, it can
bring out the best within you.

DAY 5

GOD FORGES YOU WITH FIRE

KEY TRUTH: Pressure can break you or make you.

Kyle fought cancer for ten years. A long-term battle like that can wear anyone down. Yet he took the attitude that his illness would not bury him. Every day he said, "Father, thank You that this too shall pass. Sickness cannot live in my body. My immune system is staging a comeback. My body's soldiers will win the battle."

Kyle always thought of his white blood cells as soldiers. When he was fighting cancer, his doctors "harvested" those cells so they could use them to restore his immune system after chemotherapy. When the doctors told him they needed to do their harvest in a month, Kyle asked them: "How many of my soldiers do you need to make me healthy again?"

They told him a huge number.

"I'll give you double that," Kyle promised.

Then, over the next few weeks, he prayed and prayed while envisioning a major army of white blood cell "soldiers" growing in his body. Most cancer patients take it easy during this period. He worked out on the treadmill and with weights every day.

When the doctors did their harvest, they were amazed. Kyle

gave them twice the number of white blood cells they needed. His soldiers beat the cancer.

Instead of having the victim mentality, Kyle had a victor mentality. God not only brought him out, he saw his life blossom into the fullness of what God had in store. Kyle discovered, as I have, that sometimes the things we get discouraged about are the very things God uses to promote us.

CONSIDER THIS: The only difference between a piece of black coal and a priceless diamond is the amount of pressure it has endured. How you handle your adversities will make you or break you. If you get bitter and lose your enthusiasm, you will allow the difficulties of life to bury you. Challenges can keep you from your God-given destiny unless you make the choice to shake them off and step up. When you know you are planted and not buried, you keep pressing forward with a smile on your face.

In spite of everything I shall rise again: I will take up my pencil, which I have forsaken in my great discouragement, and I will go on with my drawing.

—*Vincent van Gogh*

_____

_____

_____

_____

_____

_____

_____

WHAT THE SCRIPTURES SAY

Consider it pure joy, my brothers, whenever you face trials of many kinds, because you know that the testing of your faith develops perseverance. Perseverance must finish its work so that you may be mature and complete, not lacking anything.

—James 1:2–4 (NIV)

These things I have spoken to you, that in Me you may have peace. In the world you have tribulation, but take courage; I have overcome the world.

—John 16:33 (NASB)

A PRAYER FOR TODAY

Father, thank You for showing me that the biggest challenges and greatest disappointments are merely Your setups for my comebacks.

_____

_____

_____

> Out of defeat can come
> the best in human nature.
> As Christians face storms
> of adversity, they may rise
> with more beauty. They
> are like trees that grow on
> mountain ridges—battered
> by winds, yet trees in which
> we find the strongest wood.
>
> —*Rev. Billy Graham*

TAKEAWAY TRUTH: When you acknowledge that God is in control, it frees you to do the right thing even though the wrong thing is happening. Instead of complaining, you report victory. You say, "This problem will not defeat me. It didn't come to stay. It came to pass. I have strength for everything I need. I'm equipped, empowered, anointed. I am more than a conqueror."

DAY 6

GOD USES ADVERSITY TO STRENGTHEN YOU

KEY TRUTH: God will not allow a trial to come into your life unless He has a purpose.

God doesn't send the storms, but He uses them. When you're in difficult times, know that this challenge was not sent to destroy you. It was sent to promote you, to increase you, to strengthen you. You may not see how it will do that, at first, but God has a way. He sends adversity to bring out potential we didn't even know we had.

That's what happened to me. When my father went to be with the Lord in 1999, I felt like I had been buried in my grief. Outside of Victoria, my father was my best friend. I had worked with him closely in the ministry for seventeen years. We traveled all over the world together.

When my dad died, the wind was taken out of my sails. It was a struggle to adjust. But one thing that really helped me was a feeling down deep; I knew this sad event would not bury me. I felt, instead, that my father's passing was planting me; that somehow, someway, God would use this for my good.

There were days, though, when I thought things would never work out. I had to do like King David and just keep encouraging myself. I said, "God, I know You're still on the throne. This loss is not a surprise to You, but You still have something great in my future."

God is faithful. He brought me through that dark time. I discovered potential I didn't know was there. I did not know I could get up every Sunday and minister. The loss of my father is when my seed really blossomed. It was meant to destroy me, but God used it to increase me.

Maybe you've been through a loss and you don't see anything bright in your future. It feels like people are walking on top of you. You feel like you've been buried.

Just remember, there is a process taking place. New growth is springing forth in you—new talent, new determination, new opportunities, new friendships. God is birthing something in you greater than you are right now. Keep reminding yourself, "God is still on the throne. This is not the end. It's only the beginning."

Don't live with a chip on your shoulder. Don't dwell on your disappointments, on what didn't work out. Bitterness will keep your seed from taking root. Self-pity will hinder your growth. Self-condemnation and feeling unworthy of God's goodness will only limit how high you can go.

Shake off those feelings. Step up into faith. I've seen people go through incredible challenges with smiles on their faces. They're hoping, believing, expecting. You know what they're saying? "God, I can't wait to see what You will do next. I can't wait to see the new doors You'll open, the new friends I'll make, the new opportunities I will have."

CONSIDER THIS: If you expect that difficulty to destroy you and you give up on your dreams, then even though you're a seed with the life of Almighty God within you, even though God has already planned your comeback, because of your own thinking, it won't happen.

_____

_____

_____

_____

_____

_____

_____

_____

_____

_____

When it is dark enough,
you can see the stars.

—*Ralph Waldo Emerson*

_____

_____

_____

_____

_____

_____

_____

_____

_____

WHAT THE SCRIPTURES SAY

O Lord, you have searched me and known me. You know when I sit down and when I rise up; you discern my thoughts from far away. You search out my path and my lying down, and are acquainted with all my ways.

—Psalm 139:1–3 (NRSV)

Praise be to the God and Father of our Lord Jesus Christ! In his great mercy he has given us new birth into a living hope through the resurrection of Jesus Christ from the dead.

—1 Peter 1:3 (NIV)

A PRAYER FOR TODAY

Father in heaven, thank You for caring for me. I choose today to cast my cares on You and trust that You are working behind the scenes on my behalf. I worship and magnify You today.

_____

_____

_____

_____

_____

_____

_____

_____

_____

Before God we are never invisible, never unseen, never ignored. Our trouble and misery are seen and known for what they are—trouble and misery. God meets us in that deep distress, even when we cannot sense God's presence.

—*Mary Earle*

TAKEAWAY TRUTH: As a child of the Most High God, the Greater One lives inside of you. There are seeds of faith planted in your heart, and the way you activate those seeds is by the words of your mouth. Begin to declare, "I am bigger than this problem. I am created to overcome. I am destined to live in victory because the Greater One lives inside of me." When you speak like that, all of heaven hears you and gets behind what you are saying. So, stir up the fire that God has placed inside you. Don't just sit back and be passive. That obstacle may look impossible, but God wouldn't have allowed it in your life if He didn't already know that you could overcome it! Quit looking at your difficulties as obstacles that are going to hold you back and start looking at them as opportunities that are going to push you forward into the life of victory He has in store for you!

DAY 7

GOD KNOWS WHEN
THE TIME IS RIGHT

KEY TRUTH: You miss God's best when you give up on your promises too soon.

You must learn to trust God's timing. Often, He doesn't act as quickly as you might like. Consider that period to be a time of testing. Are you discouraged?

Are you complaining? Are you making decisions that will hinder the promise? You may have the promise in your heart. You know you've got a great future filled with hope, faith, blessings, and promotion. Yet you are impatient. You're tempted to be discouraged. You feel frustrated, maybe even inclined to make bad decisions. But God sent me to remind you of who you are and what you have on the inside. You are a child of the Most High God. You have seeds of greatness inside you.

You have royal blood flowing through your veins. You have been crowned with glory and honor. You are destined to leave your mark on this generation. It may not have happened yet, but the promise is still in you. Don't be careless toward your future. Don't make decisions that you will regret. It's easy in the heat of the moment to blow somebody off. It's easy to walk out of a marriage. It's easy on the Fridays of your life, in dark times, to think that things will never turn around.

God sent me to assure you that better days lie ahead. You will see your dreams come to pass. It may be Friday, but your Sunday is coming. When it's time for God to promote you, to vindicate you, to restore you, all the forces of darkness cannot stop good things from happening. God is looking for people who have a made-up mind; people who will trust His timing. It usually does not happen overnight, but it will happen. Abraham waited twenty years. He saw that promise come to pass. He had his son. Moses waited forty years. He came into his promise. He helped deliver God's people.

You may feel frustrated now, but God is working behind the scenes in your life. He is arranging the right people, the right breaks, and the right opportunities. Sometimes the process takes longer because not all the pieces are in place. The Scripture says that at the appointed time the promise will come to pass and it will not be one second late.

When is the appointed time? God knows when the time is right for you. When you understand this principle it takes all the pressure off. It's a very freeing way to live, knowing that as long as we stay in faith, God will release His favor, His increase, His restoration, His healing at exactly the right time in our lives.

You should not be frustrated because your dream does not become reality as soon as you would like. You should not be worried when you don't see the changes you want. Be confident that God will finish what He started. You may not see it happening, but it is on its way—God's way.

CONSIDER THIS: Your dream may be realized today, next week, next year, in five years or twenty-five years. That's okay.

Stay in faith. Know that God will bring the promise to pass and He will bring it to a flourishing finish.

_____

_____

_____

_____

_____

_____   The tragedy of life is not
                                       so much what men suffer,
_____   but rather what they miss.

_____   —*Thomas Carlyle*

_____   _____

_____

_____

_____

_____

WHAT THE SCRIPTURES SAY

There has never been the slightest doubt in my mind that the God who started this great work in you would keep at it and bring it to a flourishing finish on the very day Christ Jesus appears.

—*Philippians 1:6 (MSG)*

Do you not know that in a race all the runners run, but only one gets the prize? Run in such a way as to get the prize.

—*1 Corinthians 9:24 (NIV)*

A PRAYER FOR TODAY

Heavenly Father, thank you for your promise to complete what you've started in my life. Thank you for your faithfulness and for showing me your goodness. Give me strength to stand strong so that I can experience your fulfillment in my life today.

_____

_____

_____

All endeavor calls for the ability to tramp the last mile, shape the last plan, endure the last hours toil. The fight to the finish spirit is the one . . . characteristic we must possess if we are to face the future as finishers.

—*Henry David Thoreau*

TAKEAWAY TRUTH: God is a God of completion. He wants to finish what He's started in your life. No matter how long you've been praying, don't let the enemy tempt you into thinking that it's never going to happen. Be encouraged today because God is called the author and the finisher of your faith. That means He's working behind the scenes on your behalf. Anything He begins, any dream He puts in your heart, He is well able to finish. Stand strong on this promise. Be confident even when it looks like it's not going to happen. No matter how long it takes, stay in faith, and keep your hopes up because God has promised to finish the good work He's started in your life!

It's Time to Trust

"It's Time to Trust" builds your resolve by reminding you of those things you can trust: that all things work together for good, that God remembers you, that you can gain strength through adversity, and that there will come an anointing of ease.

DAY 1

IT'S NOT OVER UNTIL
GOD SAYS IT'S OVER

KEY TRUTH: We need to trust in God's plan.

We all experience challenges that don't make sense. Viewed in isolation, we don't understand them. But if you keep pressing forward, one day you will look back and see how each setback played into God's master plan for your life.

When we isolate negative experiences, we tend to wonder why they've happened to us. They can seem unfair and cruel, and this makes us bitter. I know people right now who are mad at God. They have no joy, no enthusiasm, because they went through a disappointment.

Instead of believing God was still in control and waiting for a new beginning, they isolated that incident. They thought, *Why did God let this happen to me?* But not everything makes sense on its own. You need to trust in God's plan. Have the attitude: "I know God has a great plan for my life. I know He is directing my steps. Even though I may not understand this, I know it's not a surprise to God. And somehow, someway, He will work it out to my advantage."

The reason God closes a door even when we're walking in obedience and being our best is because He has something better in store. But when we get sour because things don't go our way—when we are bitter, offended, and negative—that stops God from bringing His blessings.

We have to say, "God, even though I didn't get my way, I trust You. I know You know what's best for me. And I believe at the right time You will give me the desires of my heart."

Victoria and I fixed up our first house, sold it, and moved to a bigger place a few years after we were married. The people who bought our house filed a lawsuit against us after they moved in. They had a problem with the outside sewer. They not only sued us; they also sued the builder, the architect, the Realtor, the plumber, and everybody else they could think of.

We'd done nothing wrong. We were not at fault. But I was so upset over this lawsuit. The case went on for months. I had to give a deposition, and I was stressed out and nervous. It seemed like the worst thing that had ever happened to me. After the two-hour deposition, I was so nauseated I couldn't even drive home.

Then about six months later, the lawsuit was thrown out. Victoria and I were cleared. Yet I'd spent that whole six months thinking how bad things were because of the lawsuit brought against us. I kept thinking it wasn't fair. The lawsuit was just a waste of our time, I thought.

Nearly three years later, I realized what God was up to. When we signed the church's lease for the Compaq Center, some other company filed a lawsuit to prevent us from moving in. This time, I took the lawsuit in stride. I realized that God had prepared me with the legal troubles over our former house.

When I gave my deposition for the Compaq Center lawsuit, I was as calm as could be. I would not have been nearly as confident in facing this much bigger lawsuit if it hadn't been for my earlier experience. Going through tough times, you don't know what God may be preparing you for. So don't be shortsighted and think, *Oh, God. Why is this happening? This is not fair.*

God challenges you to help you grow. Know that God would not have allowed a challenge to happen if He did not plan for something good to come from it. It may be ten years before you realize the benefit that God provided.

You may be fighting a challenge right now, something that's got you stressed out. If God were to take it away, you wouldn't be prepared for what He has in store. It would keep you from reaching the level He's trying to get you to. Keep it all in perspective. That job you lost, that family member who is hard to get along with—it's not happening to you. It's happening for you. God is getting you prepared for greater levels of blessing.

Your attitude has a great impact on whether you move forward on God's path or stay put. Don't go around complaining, "God, why am I always getting these bad breaks?" Instead, stay in faith. Just say, "God, I know You're in complete control of my life. And no matter how tempted I am to be disappointed, I will not be a victim. I will not be negative, blaming other people. I know You've got me in the palm of Your hand. And I believe one day I will look out and see how this has all turned out for my benefit."

CONSIDER THIS: Just a little break, just one person, just one idea, just one touch of God's favor can turn the bitter into the sweet, sorrow into joy, mourning into dancing.

_____

_____

_____

_____

> To one who has faith, no
> explanation is necessary.
> To one without faith, no
> explanation is possible.
>
> —*St. Thomas Aquinas*

WHAT THE SCRIPTURES SAY

For I am persuaded, that neither death, nor life, nor angels, nor principalities, nor powers, nor things present, nor things to come,
Nor height, nor depth, nor any other creature, shall be able to separate us from the love of God, which is in Christ Jesus our Lord.

—*Romans 8:38–39 (KJV)*

But God, who is rich in mercy, because of His great love with which He loved us . . . raised us up together, and made us sit together in the heavenly places in Christ Jesus, that in the ages to come He might show the exceeding riches of His grace in His kindness toward us in Christ Jesus.

—*Ephesians 2:4–7 (NKJV)*

A PRAYER FOR TODAY

Father, thank You for helping me to trust in Your plan while You prepare me for greater levels of blessing.

_____

_____

_____   ———————⚮———————

_____   Faith is putting all your
_____   eggs in God's basket, then
_____   counting your blessings
_____   before they hatch.

_____   —*Ramona C. Carroll*

_____

_____

_____

_____

_____

_____

_____

TAKEAWAY TRUTH: Oftentimes, people set their focus on what God has done in the past—how He parted the Red Sea or stopped the sun for Joshua or fed thousands of people with just a little boy's small lunch. Yes, God has performed many amazing miracles throughout history; and it's important that we give Him praise, but at the same time, we also have to look forward to what God wants to do in our lives today.

(illegible)

GOD IS NOT AT A LOSS

KEY TRUTH: You can trust that in time God will turn what seems bitter into sweet.

When Moses was leading the people of Israel through the wilderness, they went day after day without water. They were so thirsty they didn't know if they could make it. They finally came to a river. They were so excited. Their dream had come true. They rushed to drink from the river, but when they tasted the water, it was bitter. They couldn't drink a drop.

Have you ever arrived somewhere, like the people of Israel, with great expectations, only to meet with disappointment? We all have had our dreams cast on the rocks of bitterness from time to time.

In 1981, we were looking forward to a big Christmas holiday with family and friends. Then, on December 11, we learned that my mother had terminal cancer. Doctors said she had just a few weeks to live. Like the people Moses was leading, we had thought we would be enjoying a family holiday, but instead we were handed sad news.

Moses' people complained to him of their thirst. The water was bitter and their lives became bitter. God told Moses to put a tree limb in the water, and when he did, those bitter waters were turned sweet. Then the people could drink freely to quench their thirst.

What is the message in this story? When life turns out bitter, when things seem unfair, God is not at a loss. He has another ingredient to turn your bitter waters into sweet.

You may not understand why you are going through difficult times. But don't try to figure it out. Faith is all about trusting God when you don't understand.

As you may know, my family's bitterness over my mother's illness also turned to relief and gratitude. With God's grace, she defied all medical expectations and beat the cancer. Her story of faith and healing has inspired many others who have done the same. God's plan has unfolded.

Some people who've experienced hardship get caught up on why God didn't answer their prayers. They grow bitter that God did not heal them or their loved one. They grow bitter because He did not restore a marriage or find them a new job right away. I've learned to never put a question mark where God has put a period. When something is over and done, let it go and move on to the next chapter in your life.

CONSIDER THIS: Instead of complaining about a bad situation, you should realize that God acts and responds to His own word. Take those promises, and remind God about what He said. Remind Him: "God, You said You're close to the brokenhearted. And I'm hurting. I've been through this disappointment. But God, You promised You would give me beauty for ashes. You said weeping endures for a night, but joy is coming." Those are promises that God is obligated to bring to pass. And when I say "obligated," I'm not saying that we're bossing God around, telling Him what to do. The principle is that God is faithful to His word. He cannot lie. It goes against His very nature. He could never break a promise. And so when we bring His promises back to Him and remind Him of what He said, it causes Him to respond.

The happiness which brings enduring worth to life is not the superficial happiness that is dependent on circumstances. It is the happiness and contentment that fills the soul even in the midst of the most distressing of circumstances and most bitter environment. It is the kind of happiness that grins when things go wrong and smiles through the tears. The happiness for which our souls ache is one undisturbed by success or failure, one which will root deeply inside us and give inward relaxation, peace, and contentment, no matter what the surface problems may be. That kind of happiness stands in need of no outward stimulus.

—*Rev. Billy Graham*

WHAT THE SCRIPTURES SAY

Do not say, "I'll pay you back for this wrong!" Wait for the LORD, and he will deliver you.

—Proverbs 20:22 (NIV)

Who is a God like you, who pardons sin and forgives the transgression of the remnant of his inheritance? You do not stay angry forever but delight to show mercy. You will again have compassion on us; you will tread our sins underfoot and hurl all our iniquities into the depths of the sea.

—Micah 7:18–19 (NIV)

A PRAYER FOR TODAY

Father, I don't understand why I am facing this trial, but rather than being bitter or angry, I thank You for the joy that is coming in the morning.

_____

_____

_____

_____

_____

_____

_____

_____

_____

_____

Recipe for greatness – To bear up under loss, to fight the bitterness of defeat and the weakness of grief, to be victor over anger, to smile when tears are close, to resist evil men and base instincts, to hate hate and to love love, to go on when it would seem good to die, to seek ever after the glory and the dream, to look up with unquenchable faith in something evermore about to be, that is what any man can do, and so be great.

—*Zane Grey*

TAKEAWAY TRUTH: God is not obligated to bring to pass what we say. But He is obligated to bring to pass what He says. This is why it's so important to find the promises that apply to your situation and remind God about what He says.

DAY 3

WRITE YOUR STORY
ACCORDING TO GOD'S PLAN

KEY TRUTH: You can determine how the next chapter is written.

The Scripture says all of our days have been written in God's book. He's already recorded every part of your life from beginning to end. God knows every disappointment, every loss, and every challenge. The good news is that your story ends in victory. Your final chapter concludes with you fulfilling your God-given destiny.

Here's the key: When you go through a disappointment, when you go through a loss, don't stop on that page. Keep moving forward. There's another chapter in front of you.

Sometimes we miss opportunities because we are so focused on what didn't work out. Whether it's a marriage that failed or a job you lost, you must leave it and move forward. You've been on that page long enough. You've reread the story 450 times. Let it go and move on to the next chapter God has written.

You may not understand everything you went through. But if you'll just keep pressing forward, not letting the bitterness take root, you will come to a chapter in your future that will pull it all together, a chapter that will make sense of it all.

Many of those who suffered hardship because of Hurricane Katrina came to Houston to recover from that terrible storm. Most of those I've met lost everything. Their lives were changed forever. Whenever I've talked with Katrina survivors, I've tried to comfort them and give them hope. I've told them that there is nothing they can do about what happened to them but that they can make a decision about how they will respond.

"You can fight it. You can resist, get bitter, and live with a chip on your shoulder. Or you can accept the hand you've been dealt, seeing this as an opportunity to meet new friends, to live in a new city, to have a new job. The choice is up to you."

Another couple I know told me recently that they'd become estranged from their son. They had had a good relationship with him. In fact, they'd worked together. But somehow they got crossways, and this son refused to speak to them. He moved to another city. They did not even have a phone number for him. They don't know how to get in touch with him. You can imagine their concern. They were discouraged. I told them that there was more to be written.

Somewhere in their future—and in yours, too—there is a restoration chapter. It may be a month, a year, or ten years, so don't get stuck on that page. Keep praying. Keep believing. Envision it. Let the seeds take root.

CONSIDER THIS: So often when difficulties come, people feel overwhelmed, unequipped, or outnumbered. They shrink back or look for an easy way out or a place to hide. But that's not God's best for us. He never intended for us to be consumed by our challenges. He intends for us to overcome them. If you're facing a difficulty today, stand strong, and show the enemy what you're made of.

_____

_____

_____

_____   ❧

_____   Life is not easy for any of us.
                              But what of that? We must
_____   have perseverance and, above
                              all, confidence in ourselves.
_____   We must believe that we are
                              gifted for something, and
_____   that this thing, at whatever
                              cost, must be attained.
_____
                                        —*Marie Curie*
_____

_____   _____

_____

_____

_____

_____

WHAT THE SCRIPTURES SAY

If God be for us, who can be against us?
—*Romans 8:31 (KJV)*

[We pray] that you may be invigorated and strengthened with
all power according to the might of His glory, [to exercise] every
kind of endurance and patience (perseverance and forbearance)
with joy.

—*Colossians 1:11 (AMP)*

A PRAYER FOR TODAY

Father in heaven, today I declare that I am determined to put You first and stand on Your promises so that I can live the life of victory You have prepared for me.

_____

_____

_____

> Failure is in a sense the highway to success, as each discovery of what is false leads us to seek earnestly after what is true.
>
> —*John Keats*

_____

_____

_____

_____

_____

_____

_____

TAKEAWAY TRUTH: Remember, you aren't alone in the fight. God is with you. He's promised never to leave you or forsake you. Just like the Scripture says, if God is for you, who can be against you? Friend, you and God are a majority. There's no weapon, no enemy, no challenge, no disease, no failure—nothing that can overtake you when God is on your side!

DAY 4

GOD WILL PUT IT ALL TOGETHER FOR YOU

KEY TRUTH: To reach up for the new, you must let go of the old.

What is behind you is not nearly as important as what lies in front of you. Everything you've been through was preparation for where you are right now. Disappointments, challenges, and failures were not meant to destroy you. They were meant to strengthen you, to build your character, to give you the fortitude to accomplish your God-given destiny.

Unfair things happen. You may not understand why hard times hit you. But you have come too far to let setbacks stop you from stepping forward. Refuse to get stuck in the past. God has a plan with your name on it, a plan full of blessing, full of favor, full of victory.

Sometimes life is like a mystery novel or a movie thriller. Things happen and we don't understand what they mean because the whole story has not been revealed. Once the final clues are given, the dots are connected, and suddenly the plot makes sense. But the story is complete only when all the pieces fall into place.

At times, we don't have all the pieces of the story God has

written for us. We don't understand how certain events in our lives will play out. We ask, Why did this happen? Why didn't my relationship work out? Why did I lose my job?

With a mystery novel or a movie thriller, you don't get frustrated. You know that eventually everything will make sense to you. You need to approach life with the same faith. Sometimes things in our lives don't make sense to us. But God's plan will be revealed to us as His plot plays out.

Something may seem unfair right now. You may be wondering, "Joel, if God is so good, why did my life turn out like this?" Or "Why did I go through that divorce?" "Why didn't I get that promotion?" "It just doesn't seem to make sense."

That frustration is due to the fact that God's plan for you is still unfolding. If you stay in faith, before long you will see how every setback, every disappointment, even a terrible loss was simply another part of your story.

CONSIDER THIS: God sees the big picture. Your life doesn't stop because of one setback or even many setbacks. Each part of your life helps advance your story. Connected and completed, they make up the whole of your life. They will come together for your fulfillment.

Any fool can count the seeds in an apple. Only God can count all the apples in one seed.

—*Robert H. Schuller*

_____

_____

_____

_____

_____

_____

_____

_____

_____

_____

WHAT THE SCRIPTURES SAY

And we know that God causes everything to work together for the good of those who love God and are called according to His purpose for them.

—Romans 8:28 (NLT)

These things I have spoken to you, that in Me you may have peace. In the world you will have tribulation; but be of good cheer, I have overcome the world.

—John 16:33 (NKJV)

A PRAYER FOR TODAY

Heavenly Father, thank You for working all things together for my good. I choose to release any doubt, any frustration, any confusion over my past, and I choose to trust in You. Help me to see the big picture as I keep my mind stayed on You.

_____

_____

_____

_____

————— ❧ —————   _____

_____

God's gifts put man's   _____
best dreams to shame.
_____
—*Elizabeth Barrett Browning*
_____

————————————————   _____

_____

_____

_____

_____

_____

_____

_____

TAKEAWAY TRUTH: You have to understand that even though life is not always fair, God is fair. He promises that He will work all things together for our good. Your life doesn't stop because of one setback. That is simply one piece of your puzzle. There is another piece coming to connect it all because God promises to work all things together for your good!

DAY 5

GOD REMEMBERS YOU

KEY TRUTH: No matter what happens, God can turn it around.

When God remembers you, He will do more than just think about you. He will show up and show out like you've never seen before. That's what happened to a young lady named Rachel in the Bible. She wanted to have a child so badly. She tried and tried but just couldn't conceive. Her womb was barren. Back in those days a woman was really looked down on if she couldn't give her husband a child. Being childless brought shame to her and her husband.

Year after year passed, and Rachel felt so alone, so empty, like she was less than she was supposed to be. To make matters worse, her sister Leah kept having baby after baby. It was like rubbing salt in the wound. But one day something happened that turned everything around. The Scripture says that "God remembered Rachel."

Isn't that phrase interesting? It doesn't say *Rachel remembered God*. And of course it's good when we reach out to God, when *we* remember *Him*. But it's even more significant when God remembers *you*.

God is so merciful. When we feel we have no more strength to believe, when we've prayed so much we can't pray any longer, when we've gotten so discouraged we just give up on the promise and think it's not meant to be, that's exactly where Rachel was. But notice what happened. God remembered her and answered her plea and gave her a child.

My friend, when God remembers you, it doesn't matter how long it's been that way. It doesn't matter how impossible it looks. God will turn it around.

You may feel like Rachel today: alone, forgotten, empty. Maybe you've given up on a dream. Maybe you have already accepted the fact that you will never have a child. You will never go back to college. You never will be successful in your finances, in your marriage. You've written off your dreams, your goals.

But understand, just because you write off your dreams doesn't mean God writes them off. God remembers you, and He remembers the dream He put within you. He remembers the goals, the promises, and your deepest desires.

CONSIDER THIS: You may have said, "Just forget about it, God." But God says, "No, no, no. I remember! I put the dream in you, and I still have a way to bring it to pass."

_____

_____

_____

_____

_____

_____

_____

_____

_____

_____   ⚜

_____   _____

_____   A dream is your creative vision
                         for your life in the future. A
_____   goal is what specifically you
                         intend to make happen. Dreams
_____   and goals should be just out of
                         your present reach but not out
_____   of sight. Dreams and goals are
                         coming attractions in your life.
_____
                                    —*Joseph Campbell*
_____
                         _____

_____

_____

WHAT THE SCRIPTURES SAY

"I will give you back your health and heal your wounds," says
the Lord.

                                    —*Jeremiah 30:17 (NLT)*

I AM THE Lord, the God of all the peoples of the world. Is anything too hard for me?

                                    —*Jeremiah 32:27 (NLT)*

A PRAYER FOR TODAY

Father, thank You for remembering me and helping me. I put
my trust in Your unfailing love.

_____

_____

_____

_____

_____

————————— ❧ —————————

> Always dream and shoot
> higher than you know
> you can do. Don't bother
> just to be better than
> your contemporaries or
> predecessors. Try to be
> better than yourself.
>
> —*William Faulkner*

_____

_____

_____

_____

_____

_____

_____

_____

_____

_____

_____

_____

_____

TAKEAWAY TRUTH: No matter how troubled your life may be, God can get help to you. It may not come when you want it or expect it, but He will take you from the miry clay and set your feet on solid ground.

DAY 6

GOD CAN TURN BAD TIMES INTO BLESSED DAYS

KEY POINT: We serve a God who is not limited to the natural.

Jake, a man of little faith, was hiking through the woods. He was caught in a terrible snowstorm. The storm was so blinding, Jake lost all sense of direction. It was quickly getting dark. He wasn't an experienced hiker. He didn't have the proper gear. He was just out trying to get some exercise. He knew he couldn't survive all night in the cold.

Disoriented and exhausted, he could not keep walking. He found a small crevice in a rock wall and took shelter there. To his surprise, he woke up the next morning as warm as toast. When he regained his senses, he realized that this huge shaggy dog was curled up beside him. That dog acted just like a big heater. He had no idea where the dog came from. But it saved his life.

Up to that point, Jake had little interest in matters of faith. Now he is outspoken about his beliefs. He even has a ministry. Everywhere he goes, Jake tells people that when all else was lost, God remembered him.

You may have written off your dreams. You may have given

up on promises God put in your heart. But God has not forgotten you. He can always turn bad times into blessed days.

If you were to lose your job, God may give you a better job with better benefits, making better money. So do not feel abandoned. If someone you care for walks out of your life, know that God can walk someone more worthy right back in. Do not ever feel abandoned. God remembers you. He remembers the dreams He's placed on the inside. He remembers the destiny He created for you. He remembers the assignment you've been given.

Critics and foes may try to push you down. You may be tempted to feel alone and forgotten. But fight those feelings. Go through your days thanking God for remembering you. God knows every lonely night, and He sees every tear you've ever shed. When life deals you a tough blow, when you pray but the heavens are silent, you need to remind yourself of this promise: "God has not forgotten about me, my hopes, or my dreams. He's promised He'll pay me back double."

CONSIDER THIS: All those seeds that you've sown—it's just a matter of time before you reap your harvest. We serve a God who is not limited to the natural. You have an assignment and destiny to fulfill. No matter how bad it looks or how many obstacles are in your path, God has not forgotten about you. He is not going to take away His calling on your life. You may be far away from where you know in your heart God wants you to be, but you might as well get ready, because the Most High God is not going to write you off. And when God remembers you, all the forces of darkness cannot keep you from fulfilling your purpose. A disappointment, a sickness, or a person can't stop it; there is nothing that can keep you from your destiny.

_____

_____

_____   ———————— ❧ ————————

_____
                                        By the power of faith
_____   every enduring work
                                        is accomplished.
_____
                                        —*James Allen*
_____
                                        ————————————————
_____

_____

_____

_____

_____

_____

_____

WHAT THE SCRIPTURES SAY

For the LORD your God is a merciful God; he will not aban-
don or destroy you or forget the covenant with your forefathers,
which he confirmed to them by oath.

—*Deuteronomy 4:31 (NIV)*

He remembers his covenant forever, the word he commanded,
for a thousand generations.

—*Psalm 105:8 (NIV)*

A PRAYER FOR TODAY

Father, thank You for remembering Your promises. You're remembering my dreams. You're remembering my destiny.

_____

_____

_____

_____

❧

Believe it is possible to
solve your problem.
Tremendous things happen
to the believer. So believe the
answer will come. It will.

—*Norman Vincent Peale*

_____

_____

_____

_____

_____

_____

_____

_____

_____

_____

_____

TAKEAWAY TRUTH: It's easy in life to feel that we're forgotten, that our hopes and dreams don't matter. People may leave you when you need them the most, but God is the friend who sticks closer than a brother.

DAY 7

GOD IS ALL YOU NEED

KEY TRUTH: Your challenges are meant to promote you.

Moses was in the desert leading two million people, trying to get them to the Promised Land. They didn't have any equipment. They didn't have any swords or shields. They had just come out of slavery. They weren't even trained to fight. How were they supposed to protect themselves? It looked like they could be easily conquered by their enemies. One day Moses was very discouraged. People were complaining to him. He was just about ready to give up. And God said, "Moses, what do you have in your hand?"

He was holding a rod. He said in effect, "Oh nothing, God. Just an old stick—something I picked up along the way."

God said, "Throw it down on the ground."

Moses threw it down and it turned into a snake.

God said, "Pick it up."

Moses picked it up and it turned back into a rod.

What was God saying?

"You have whatever you need. It may look like a rod, but if it needs to be a key to open a door, I'll turn it into a key. If it needs to be a shield to protect you, I'll turn it into a shield. If it needs to be healing to restore you, I'll turn it into that."

Quit looking at what you don't have. God is saying, *"I can become what you need."*

During World War II, a U.S. marine was separated from his unit during intense fighting. The smoke was so heavy, he became disoriented. He lost all contact with his comrades. He was alone in the jungle. He could hear the enemy soldiers getting closer and closer.

Then the marine saw a cliff riddled with caves. He ran to it and hid in a cave, hoping he wouldn't be found. There, he prayed for God's help and protection. As the soldier prayed, a spider dropped down over the entry of the cave and began spinning a web.

The marine had to laugh, despite his fears. "God, I need a brick wall, and You send me a spider?"

Still, as the spider created a thick web of many layers, the battlefield grew silent. The marine sat there for hours and hours. Then he heard enemy soldiers checking nearby caves. He braced himself for his final stand. But when the enemy came to his cave, one of them noticed the huge spiderweb over the entry.

"We don't need to check in here," he said. "No one could have gone in without disturbing this web."

God supernaturally protected that marine's life. He later asked for God's forgiveness.

"When I saw that spider, I laughed," he said. "But now I realize with You a spider's web can be stronger than a brick wall."

He has everything you need. And even if He doesn't have it, He can create it. He can cause a spider to spin a web and keep you out of trouble. He can cause one smooth stone to hit a giant and bring him down. God is in complete control.

So know that adversity in your life was never meant to defeat you. It was meant to promote you. When you have a problem, it's easy to think, "This is too big. I can't do it. It's just too much."

But understand that God never matches the problem to the size of the person. He matches it to the size of your destiny. So if you're facing a big challenge, keep it in the right perspective.

Don't get discouraged. Be encouraged. That's simply God setting you up for a major promotion, major increase. If you run from your problems and turn negative and sour, really, you're running from your destiny. If you'll learn to run to your problem, face it in faith knowing that God is in control, knowing that He can become what you need, then you are running to your destiny.

Isn't it interesting that after Goliath is defeated, we don't hear anything more about him? I believe that Goliath was created for David's purpose. He was created to establish David as a great man.

In the same way, the major challenges you encounter are put in your path to promote you. They are there so you can show who you really are. When others see God's favor on your life, when they see you rise above adversity, when they see you accomplish your God-given dreams, you honor God and prove His anointing in your life.

Your critics may think you don't deserve your dreams. They may think you are not talented or even doctrinally correct. But one thing for sure, when you defeat a Goliath, no one can doubt that God's favor is on you.

When Jesus healed a blind man, the religious crowd got all upset. They argued over why he was healed and how he was healed. They wondered who was to blame for him being blind in the first place. The debate went on and on.

Finally, the blind man said, "Listen, you are confusing me. I can't answer all of your questions. All I can tell you is this: I was blind, but now I can see."

He was saying, "The proof of the pudding is in the eating. You can argue all day long, but the fact is I can see because of God's goodness in my life."

CONSIDER THIS: Some today think we're not supposed to be blessed. Some think that God does not want us to prosper and live in victory. But the problem with that is it's too late to convince me, because God has already blessed me. He's already prospered me. He's already opened up supernatural doors.

The man who removes a mountain begins by carrying away small stones.

—*William Faulkner*

WHAT THE SCRIPTURES SAY

Rejoice in the Lord, you [consistently] righteous (upright and in right standing with God), and give thanks at the remembrance of His holiness.

—Psalm 97:12 (AMP)

Give praise and thanks to the Lord of hosts, for the Lord is good; for His mercy and kindness and steadfast love endure forever! For I will cause the captivity of the land to be reversed and return to be as it was at first, says the Lord.

—Jeremiah 33:11 (AMP)

A PRAYER FOR TODAY

Father in heaven, I come to you today giving you all that I am. I choose to praise you no matter what is going on. Fill my heart with joy, and help me see the bright future You have in store for me.

_____

_____

_____

_____

_____

_____

_____

_____

The strongest oak tree of the
forest is not the one that is
protected from the storm and
hidden from the sun. It's the one
that stands in the open where it
is compelled to struggle for its
existence against the winds and
rains and the scorching sun.

—*Napoleon Hill*

TAKEAWAY TRUTH: No matter what is going on, when you stay full of joy and praise, God is going to turn things around in your favor. He is going to reverse negative situations. He's going to restore things you thought were lost for good! But notice it doesn't happen by complaining or being negative or sour. It happens when you have the voice of gladness, the voice of joy. So go out each day with a smile on your face. Things may not always go your way, but don't get discouraged. Shake it off and count it all joy. When you live with this attitude, you might as well get ready—God is going to reverse and restore every area of your life!

It's Time to Stretch

We stretch to grow. We stretch to build strength. We stretch to reach beyond previous levels of accomplishment and fulfillment. The final chapters will motivate you to step into your divine destiny, to stay open for something new, to find your place of blessing, and to believe for a supernatural year.

DAY 1

YOU ARE FULLY EQUIPPED

KEY TRUTH: God gave you all you need to fulfill your destiny.

God matched you with your world, your circumstances, and your environment. He decided what your purpose would be in that world. He gave you an assignment to fulfill. Then He granted you the gifts, the talents, the looks, the creativity, the personality to get the job done. He equipped you with exactly what you need. If you needed to be taller, God would have made you taller. If you needed language skills, God gave them to you. If you needed musical talent, God granted that gift to you.

Do not take for granted any of your gifts. Do not complain about those you wish you had. You are fearfully and wonderfully made. God made you fully loaded and totally equipped. He chose your features in the same way that you select a car. You can purchase a car totally stripped down. Just the basics. No air-conditioning. No power windows. No radio. Just a standard car.

But know this: When God made you, He had all the options put on. You are not a want-to-be. You are not a stripped-down version of the real thing. You are fully loaded and totally equipped.

When God created you, He said, "I want the deluxe package. I want the chrome wheels. I want the sun roof. I want the navigation. I want the stereo with surround. And, oh yeah, don't forget my pinstripes."

Some of you got a sedan. Some of you got a compact. Some of you got a truck. Some of you got a low rider. Don't be discouraged even if you got a station wagon, like my brother, Paul.

Whatever God has given you, He made you fully loaded and totally equipped. I realize I may not have what someone else has. He may be a Ferrari, and I'm a Ford. But I'm not the least bit worried. I know I have what I need to fulfill my purpose.

It's when we try to be something we're not that life gets frustrating. I've learned it's easy to be me. I don't have to perform. I don't have to manipulate things. I can just relax and be myself.

Do you know I can be a better me than anybody else in the whole world? Why? I'm anointed to be me. You are anointed to be you. Nobody can beat you at being you. Quit worrying about what you don't have. Instead, be the best you that you can possibly be.

When I first started ministering, I was very intimidated, very unsure of myself. I would hear other ministers who were so dynamic. Many of them could not only speak exceptionally well, but they could even sing incredibly well. At the end of their sermons, they'd just burst out into song, and they were so effective, they'd almost give you chill bumps. I'd think, *God, why can't I sing like that? Why don't I have their gift?*

But one day I realized God has given me what I need. If they have it and I don't, it must mean that I don't need it. And, yes, they may be able to sing exceptionally well, but I know this: Their jokes aren't as good as mine.

CONSIDER THIS: You are fully loaded and totally equipped. Don't you dare go around thinking, *Oh, I don't have what it* *takes.* No, you go around saying, "I am anointed. I am empowered. I am talented. I am creative. I am a fully loaded person."

_____

_____

_____   ———————— ⚬ ————————

_____   To begin to think with
                                    purpose, is to enter the ranks
_____   of those strong ones who only
                                    recognize failure as one of
_____   the pathways to attainment.

_____   —*James Allen*

_____   _____

_____

_____

_____

_____

WHAT THE SCRIPTURES SAY

But he who did not know, yet committed things deserving of stripes, shall be beaten with few. For everyone to whom **much is given**, from him **much** will be required; and to whom **much** has been committed, of him they will ask the more.

—*Luke 12:48 (NKJV)*

Time and chance happen to them all.
—*Ecclesiastes 9:11 (NIV)*

A PRAYER FOR TODAY

Father God, thank You for the good things You have in store for my future. Thank You for Your peace and joy that surround my every step. I choose today to keep my heart focused on those good things ahead.

Hide not your talents. They for use were made. What's a sundial in the shade?

—*Benjamin Franklin*

TAKEAWAY TRUTH: So many people miss out on the good things because they allow fear to distract them and hold them back. They say, "What if I fail?" "What if they don't like me?" "What if I make a mistake?" To that I say, "What if you succeed?" "What if they like you?" "What if you do it better than anyone else?" That's expecting God's goodness and favor. And when you go out each day with an attitude of faith and expectancy, you'll see those good things He has in store. You'll walk into divine moments of favor, moments of blessing, moments of increase; and you'll be fully equipped to live the life of victory!

ROLL AWAY THE STONE AND GOD WILL DO THE REST

KEY TRUTH: If you will see yourself as a person of God-given destiny and stretch your faith, God will show up and show out in amazing ways.

In the Scripture, when Lazarus died, Jesus said to the disciples, "Roll away the stone and I'll raise Lazarus." It's interesting: Jesus could have rolled away the stone. Here Jesus was about to raise a dead man. But it was the principle; God expects us to do what we can, and then He will do what we can't.

If you will do the natural, God will do the supernatural. If you will do the ordinary, God will do the extraordinary. But God will not do for you what you can do for yourself.

Let me ask you: Are you rolling away the stone? Do you make work on time each day? Are you giving it your best? Are you productive? Do you have a good attitude? If you will do what you can, God will do what you cannot.

Maybe you're single and you have a desire to get married. You cannot sit at home every night watching television praying that Miss America will come knocking on your door. You need to get out and meet some new friends. Go to the mall. Get some new clothes. Dress better. Look better.

You are a fully loaded person. You have a lot to offer. When somebody marries you, they're getting a prize. You are extremely valuable. You have the fingerprints of God all over you. But you've got to see yourself the right way.

"Joel, I'm kind of shy. I'm reserved."

So am I, but I stand in front of thousands of people every week. Do you know how much nerve it took me to even call Victoria and ask her out on our first date? It took me two weeks to get my courage up. I finally convinced myself that I am a fully loaded person and she would be absolutely crazy to say no to me. I called her. She said yes and I nearly passed out.

After twenty-three years of marriage, I can tell you that Victoria is fully loaded and totally equipped. She's one of a kind. My point is that when you make a move, God will make a move. You do the natural, and God will do the supernatural. You may be stuck in your comfort zone. You're a fully loaded person using about ten percent of what God has given you. I want to stir you out of complacency.

If you are not uncomfortable once in a while, then you're not really using your faith. Faith is all about stretching. Your obstacles, challenges, and opportunities may seem intimidating, but God would not have presented them to you if He had not known already that you have what it takes.

Before you were born, God knew you. He has planned out all your days for good. Believe in His plan for you. Don't let your potential lie dormant. Share your gifts with the world. You have more in you than you realize. There is talent you've not yet discovered. You may have had some great victories in your past, but that is nothing compared to what God has in your future.

I know you are not average. You are not ordinary. I'm declaring that the treasure buried in you will come out. I'm calling forth the dreams, the gifts, the talents, the businesses, the ideas, the inventions, the books, the songs, the movies. I'm calling forth your untapped potential.

When you push yourself to make full use of your God-given gifts, you will develop a confidence to do things you wouldn't do before. You will feel a supernatural strength. Supernatural doors will open up for you. Supernatural opportunities are coming your way. Don't shrink back. Don't be intimidated. The Creator of the universe has not only equipped and empowered you; He's also breathing in your direction. He's breathing creativity. He's breathing confidence. He's breathing ideas. He's breathing restoration.

God is saying to you what He said to Joshua: "Be strong and of good courage . . . for the Lord your God is with you."

You may have been told a thousand times what you can't do. But I'm here to tell you what you can do. You can overcome every obstacle. You can prosper in spite of the economy. You can be healthy and whole once again. You can recover from a fall. You can become all that God created You to be.

CONSIDER THIS: If you don't understand who you are, then you'll never have the confidence to get out of your comfort zone and take steps of faith. This is imperative to fulfilling your destiny. I've learned that when I make a move, God will make a move. When I get out of my comfort zone and stretch my faith, then God will release more of my favor. When I think bigger, God will act bigger. When I believe I can rise higher and I put my shoulders back and I hold my head up high and walk like I'm a child of the most high God, that is when God shows up and shows out in unusual ways.

_____

_____

_____

_____

———— ❧ ————   _____

_____

There is no greater agony   _____
than bearing an untold
story inside you.   _____

—*Maya Angelou*   _____

————————   _____

_____

_____

_____

WHAT THE SCRIPTURES SAY

Jesus, once more deeply moved, came to the tomb. It was a cave
with a stone laid across the entrance. "Take away the stone," he
said.

"But, Lord," said Martha, the sister of the dead man, "by this
time there is a bad odor, for he has been there four days."

Then Jesus said, "Did I not tell you that if you believed, you
would see the glory of God?"

—John 11:38–40 (NIV)

Have not I commanded thee? Be strong and of a good courage;
be not afraid, neither be thou dismayed: for the LORD thy God
is with thee whithersoever thou goest.

—Joshua 1:9 (KJV)

A PRAYER FOR TODAY

Father, fill me with Your confidence and assurance to embrace everything You have for me.

_____

_____

_____

_____

_____

_____

_____

_____

_____

_____

_____

_____

_____

_____

There is a need to find and sing our own song, to stretch our limbs and shake them in a dance so wild that nothing can roost there, that stirs the yearning for solitary wings.

—*Barbara Lazear Ascher*

TAKEAWAY TRUTH: God's desire is that we continually progress, that we reach higher heights and go to new levels. Oftentimes, as soon as we make the decision to step out in faith and obey God, the enemy brings in fear to try to stop us. He'll do his best to use fear to try to convince us to shrink back and stay where we are. The Bible says that fear is a spirit. It plays on our emotions and holds us back. But the good news is that we have power over fear! Scripture says that perfect love casts out all fear. When we receive God's perfect love, we will have confidence about the future, because we know His plans are for our good. Today, choose to believe God's word and receive His love so that you can overcome fear and move forward into the good life He has prepared for you!

DAY 3

GOD MAKES OUR
ORDINARY EXTRAORDINARY

KEY TRUTH: Dare to dream big. Think big. Believe big.

Police officer Julia Burney-Witherspoon patrolled a very rough area of her hometown, Racine, Wisconsin. The oldest of twelve, she'd taught her brothers and sisters to read. She'd always wanted to help other children read, too.

When sent on police calls to troubled homes, she often noticed that the children had no books to read. This just broke her heart. She wanted to do something about it. But what could she do? She had limited resources.

Instead of giving up and thinking it would never happen, she kept hoping, praying, and believing. Then, one night, she answered a false alarm at this huge warehouse. When she flipped the lights on, she saw thousands of children's books just waiting to be destroyed. They were brand-new but they had been discarded because they had little imperfections.

"When I saw those books, I knew they were mine," Officer Burney-Witherspoon said.

She asked the warehouse owner if she could have the imperfect books. "Fine, they're all yours," he said.

At first, the policewoman and her fellow officers tried to distribute the books from their patrol cars. Eventually she raised the money to open a community reading center where children and their parents could come.

What happened? The Master stepped in. God made a way where it looked like there was no way. When you live a life of excellence and integrity, a life that's pleasing to the Lord, God will bring your dreams to pass. He will cause you to be at the right place at the right time. You will find yourself even stumbling into God's blessings. Like Officer Burney-Witherspoon, you may not have the resources right now. But that's okay. God does.

CONSIDER THIS: As you take steps toward your divine destiny, God will release more of His favor. Don't be surprised when things fall into place.

Our greatest glory is not in never failing, but in rising up every time we fail.

—*Ralph Waldo Emerson*

_____

_____

_____

_____

_____

_____

WHAT THE SCRIPTURES SAY

Run in such a way as to get the prize.

—1 Corinthians 9:24 (NIV)

Therefore put on the full armor of God, so that when the day of evil comes, you may be able to stand your ground, and after you have done everything, to stand.

—Ephesians 6:13 (NIV)

A PRAYER FOR TODAY

Father, today I choose to stand strong in You. Today I choose to run my race with conviction—strong until the end. I choose to forget the past and press forward into the destiny You have in store for me.

_____

_____

_____

_____

_____

_____

_____

_____

❧

_____

Problems are not stop
signs, they are guidelines.

—*Robert H. Schuller*   _____

_____

_____   _____

_____

_____

_____

_____

_____

TAKEAWAY TRUTH: Today, if there's a dream in your heart, something you believe in—a relationship turnaround, a business opportunity, overcoming an addiction—keep pursuing it! Run the race to win the prize! Don't settle until you see the fullness of what God has placed in your heart. As you stand strong in your faith, I believe God will pour out His favor and blessing upon you, and you will see the victory He has in store for you!

DAY 4

MAKE THE HIGHEST MARK

KEY TRUTH: When you are willing to always strive to do your best, to fulfill your highest potential, God will reward you.

A professor at a major university was about to pass out the final exam, the most important test of the year for his class. But first, he told his students how proud he was of them, how disciplined they had been, and how they just worked so hard.

Since they had done so well, he made them a special offer. He said, "Anyone who would like to get an automatic C on this test, just raise your hand, and you don't even have to take the test. I'll just give you a C."

One hand went up. Then another, and another, and another until about half of the class had opted out of taking the test. Those students received the automatic C. They were so happy. They left full of joy.

The professor then passed out tests to the rest of the students. He placed the forms on their desks and asked them not to turn them over until instructed to do so. For the next few minutes, he encouraged them and told how they would do great things in life. He congratulated them for not settling for a mediocre grade. "You are willing to strive to do your best, to fulfill your highest potential, and you will be rewarded for that all of your lives," he said.

Then the professor gave his students the okay to turn their tests over and begin. Well, they discovered their tests had just two short sentences: "Congratulations. You've just made an A."

Too often, we take the easy way out. We sit back and settle for mediocrity when we should strive and stretch to develop our potential. *Hey, a C is not so bad*, we think. *I'm doing okay.* Maybe so, but you have more in you. Don't take the easy way out. Keep growing. Keep learning. Stir up the gifts inside. Put a demand on your potential. That's the only way it will be released.

CONSIDER THIS: God did not create you to be average. He created you to excel! Not only has He chosen you, but He has equipped you with everything you need to live His abundant life. He has deposited seeds of greatness inside every person. But in order to tap into those seeds of greatness, you have to believe this and act on it. Know your value and strive to fulfill God's plan for you. When you do that, you will rise up higher and higher into the life of victory He has prepared for you!

Success seems to be connected to action. Successful people keep moving. They make mistakes, but they never quit.

—*J. Willard Marriott*

_____

_____

_____

_____

_____

_____

_____

_____

WHAT THE SCRIPTURES SAY

For He chose us in Him before the creation of the world.
—*Ephesians 1:4 (NIV)*

Whatever you do, work at it with all your heart, as working for the Lord, not for men.
—*Colossians 3:23 (NIV)*

A PRAYER FOR TODAY

Father God, thank You for choosing me. Thank You for equipping me. Help me to see myself the way You see me. Show me Your ways that I may walk with You in confidence and trust all the days of my life.

_____

_____

_____

_____

The only thing I had was this recipe, and with that recipe was a dream. And those were the only things that I had to build my business: a recipe and a dream. And there was no way, no way, I wasn't going to see this dream through.

—*Debbi Fields*

TAKEAWAY TRUTH: Dream big, and if one dream dies, dream another dream. Don't settle for mediocrity. We serve a God who is above and beyond anything we can think of. There's nothing you can dream of that God can't do. Ask Him to bring you the right people, the right opportunities, and the right resources. As you follow His lead in your heart, I believe you'll move forward and see every dream and desire come to pass in Jesus' name!

DAY 5

GOD WANTS YOU TO
EMBRACE THE POSSIBILITIES

KEY TRUTH: Limited thinking brings a limited life, so we should be open to creating the best lives we possibly can.

There was once this professional thief. He was incredibly talented. He was brilliant. Not that I'm considering a new line of work, but the way he planned his burglaries was fascinating. He burglarized homes for twenty-one years without being caught. He never hurt anyone. He only broke in during the day if no one was home. The police were so frustrated. They had figured out his pattern and they knew, generally, where he would hit, but he always outsmarted them. They brought in federal agents and some of the most brilliant detectives around. But still, year after year, he continued to elude them.

Then, because of a fluke, he was caught. I saw an interview with him. He looked like a typical middle-class businessman. He did not look like a thief. An interviewer asked him, "With all of your skills and expertise, why did you choose a life of crime?"

I'll never forget the way he answered. "This is all that I know how to do," he said. The thief explained that he was raised in a dysfunctional family. He said he didn't have anyone to guide him. Yet there have been many people who have risen above their circumstances to become successful and to make the world a better place.

As I watched his interview, I thought, *How limited some people become in their thinking. They can't see beyond their circumstances to the possibilities.* I wanted to say to the thief, "If you could steal successfully for twenty-one years, outsmarting some of the brightest minds around, don't you think you could run your own business? Don't you think you could do something equally as successful while being productive with your life?"

I worry about such limited thinking. I see it often. A young man came to me after a service and told me that selling drugs was all he knew how to do. He came from a very rough neighborhood. "Joel, I don't like what I do, but I don't have any other skills," he said. "I've never been to college. This is the only way I know how to make a living."

I said, "Listen, if you can sell drugs, don't sell yourself short. You're a lot smarter than you think. That's not the only thing you can do. Think about it like this: If you can sell drugs, you have to know how to market your product; that's marketing. You have to know how to get the word out; that's advertising. You have to take care of your clients; that's customer service. You have to know when to sell and when not to sell; that's a management decision. Don't fool yourself. If you can sell drugs, you can sell medical equipment. You can sell electronics. You can sell stocks and bonds."

CONSIDER THIS: Don't use your God-given talents for the wrong purposes. Embrace the possibilities for your life, and put your talents to their highest use. Let me tell you, you have a gift. You have something to offer. Don't get stuck with the mind-set that *This is all I know how to do for the rest of my life.* Open your mind to the greatest possibilities. Then you'll see God begin to open up new doors. It's not too late. You're not too old. You haven't made too many mistakes. You wouldn't be here if God didn't have more for you to accomplish.

_____

_____

_____   _____

_____

_____   The greater the difficulty, the
                                    more glory in surmounting
_____   it. Skillful pilots gain
                                    their reputation from
_____   storms and tempests.

_____   —*Epictetus*

_____   _____

_____

_____

_____

WHAT THE SCRIPTURES SAY

This is why I remind you to fan into flames the spiritual gift God gave you when I laid my hands on you.

—*2 Timothy 1:6 (NLT)*

Some trust in chariots and some in horses, but we trust in the name of the Lord our God.

—*Psalm 20:7 (NIV)*

A PRAYER FOR TODAY

Father, I trust that with You all things are possible. Today, I take my eyes off my circumstances, and I choose to put my trust and hope in You. I honor You and thank You for Your faithfulness.

Reflect upon your blessings, of which every man has plenty, not on your past misfortunes, of which all men have some.

—*Charles Dickens*

TAKEAWAY TRUTH: Sometimes, it's easy to get discouraged when circumstances are difficult. Often, there are things you can't control. Maybe you aren't getting out of debt as fast as you wanted. Or you're experiencing some challenges in your health or relationships. Still, you don't have to limit yourself to just accepting what happens to you. That's putting God in a box.

Just because it hasn't happened yet doesn't mean it isn't going to happen. Remember, we serve a supernatural God. When we believe, all things become possible! There may not be a way in the natural, but that's okay. God can do what men can't do. Trust God to make a way. He'll part the waters if He has to! He'll do whatever it takes to lead and guide you in the path of victory that He has prepared for you!

DAY 6

FIND GOD'S HIGHEST PATH FOR YOUR LIFE

KEY TRUTH: God's dream for your life is so much bigger, so much greater than your own.

I heard about this little boy, five or six years old, who picked up his baseball and bat one day and said to himself, "I am the best hitter in all the world." He threw the ball up, took a swing, and missed. He picked the ball up and said it more determinedly: "I am the best hitter in all the world." He threw it up and swung. *Strike two.* Missed again.

He picked the ball up. This time he straightened his hat. He said it with even more intensity: "I am the best hitter in all the world." He threw the ball up, concentrated the best he could, took a swing, and he missed. *Strike three.*

He simply laid his bat down, picked the ball up, and said, "What do you know? I am the best *pitcher* in all the world."

CONSIDER THIS: If you are to be successful, you must remain open to new ideas. Be willing to reinvent yourself. The Scripture says in Isaiah 55:8 that God's ways are not our ways. They are higher and better than our ways. That tells me God's dream for your life is so much bigger, so much greater than your own.

When a door closes, something doesn't work out, don't sit around in self-pity thinking, *Poor old me.* No, we may have a reason to feel sorry for ourselves, but we don't have a right. God is still on the throne. He still has a plan.

Man is a goal-seeking animal.
His life only has meaning
if he is reaching out and
striving for his goals.

—*Aristotle*

WHAT THE SCRIPTURES SAY

"My thoughts are nothing like your thoughts," says the LORD.
"And my ways are far beyond anything you could imagine.
For just as the heavens are higher than the earth,
so my ways are higher then your ways
and my thoughts higher than your thoughts."

—*Isaiah 55:8–9 (NLT)*

Set your minds on things above, not on earthly things.

—*Colossians 3:2 (NIV)*

A PRAYER FOR TODAY

Father, thank You that I am blessed and highly favored. I am above only and not beneath, I am the head and not the tail. I am the victor, not a victim. I am righteous, and my path shines brighter and brighter to the full day. I am more than a conqueror through Christ Jesus.

_____

_____

_____

_____

_____

_____   Man's reach should exceed his
                                          grasp, or what's a heaven for?

_____   —*Robert Browning*

_____

_____

_____

_____

_____

_____

_____

TAKEAWAY TRUTH: God wants to bless you indeed, and enlarge your territory. His way and thoughts are so much higher than ours, and His plan is so much bigger than we can imagine. Choose today to focus on the good things God has in store for you. Don't allow difficult circumstances to wear you down into negativity. Choose to think God's thoughts by meditating on His word.

POSITION YOURSELF FOR GOD'S ANOINTING

KEY TRUTH: Your destiny is connected to being in the right place, God's place of blessing.

In the Old Testament, God promised Elisha that he would have a double portion of Elijah's anointing. But God said, "Elisha, it will happen under one condition, not how much you pray, not how many scriptures you can quote. You have to be in the right place. You have to stay close to Elijah."

For years Elisha was faithful. He followed Elijah everywhere he went. In fact, a couple of times Elijah tried to get rid of him, tried to lose him. But Elisha stayed right with him. He was determined.

Elisha's job was to help take care of Elijah, who was an older man. He would take him food and water, assist him in menial things. In the natural, his work appeared to be unimportant. I'm sure some of Elisha's friends said, "Elisha, what are you doing spending your time following this older man around? You've got dreams and desires. You need to get on with your life."

But Elisha knew something they didn't know. He knew how important it was to be in the right place. He knew that at the right time, God would release double the blessings into his life.

He knew if he stayed close to Elijah, little by little, that same anointing would flow into him.

Sometimes it may be difficult for you, just as it was for Elisha. You think, *I'm serving, and nobody appreciates what I do. I work and get nothing in return.*

Yet, whether you realize it or not, God's anointing will flow upon you. Elisha was faithful. Because he recognized his destiny and connected to the right place, he received exactly what God promised: a double portion.

When you are in the right place, connected to the right person, that's when God will release great things into your life. Look for the signs in your own life. Be determined to reach the highest place of blessing. Search your heart. Make sure you are obeying. Stay faithful.

Remember, your blessing is connected to being in the right place physically, emotionally, mentally, and spiritually. If you make staying in God's perfect will a priority, God will lead you and guide you. He will pour out His blessings and favor, and you'll live that life of victory He has in store for you.

CONSIDER THIS: It's important to put yourself in a position to receive good advice, wise mentoring, and all of God's blessings. So stay faithful, and know that God's blessing is available to you. Your destiny is connected to being in the right place, God's place of blessing. Stay faithful, and God will double your blessings.

What this power is I cannot
say; all I know is that it exists
and it becomes available
only when a man is in that
state of mind in which he
knows exactly what he wants
and is fully determined not
to quit until he finds it.

—*Alexander Graham Bell*

WHAT THE SCRIPTURES SAY

When they came to the other side, Elijah said to Elisha, "Tell me what I can do for you before I am taken away."

And Elisha replied, "Please let me inherit a double share of your spirit and become our successor."

—*2 Kings 2:9 (NLT)*

I am writing these things to warn you about those who want to lead you astray. But you have received the Holy Spirit, and he lives within you, so you don't need anyone to teach you what is true. For the Spirit teaches you everything you need to know, and what he teaches is true—it is not a lie. So just as he has taught you, remain in fellowship with Christ.

—*1 John 2:26–27 (NLT)*

A PRAYER FOR TODAY

Father, thank You for giving me a double portion of Your blessing. I am anointed to fulfill my destiny!

_____

_____

_____

_____

—✦—

Far better it is to dare mighty
things, to win glorious
triumphs, even though
checkered by failure, than to
take rank with those poor
spirits who neither enjoy nor
suffer too much, because they
live in the gray twilight that
knows not victory nor defeat.

—*Theodore Roosevelt*

TAKEAWAY TRUTH: The Bible tells us that God inhabits the praises of His people. His presence manifests itself wherever you are when you worship Him. God will open opportunities for you and bring you divine connections to change your life in ways you cannot imagine.